SHEA BART ANDREONE

CARRY ON

Contents

Introduction

A s the youngest of three, with a large age gap between the next oldest sibling and me, I often felt like an only child. I begged my parents to have a fourth child, a younger sibling for me. Their response was often to smile, giggle, or just say, "We are sorry, but you are going to be our last baby."

I loved little kids from a young age, and if I couldn't have a baby sibling, I wanted to babysit. I was nine when I remember asking a family friend if I could babysit her eight-month-old. She let me help by giving her baby girl walks in her stroller, letting me feed her, and sometimes I would get to hold her on my hip, which made me feel really grown up. My first paying job was of course babysitting, and then I went on to be a day camp counselor, and even my minor in college was early education.

I always knew I wanted to be a mama. I always knew from a young age that I wanted to have my own babies one day. I always saw my future with children as a part of it, so when I finally met someone I wanted to become a parent with, I was shocked when we tried to conceive that it did not happen right away. My entire identity as an adult was predicated on children being a part of my life, so I did not know what to do with the knowledge that this choice to have a child was maybe not in my control.

My husband and I both shared the desire to start a family, so we researched and tried different options hoping for success. It took time, money, and a lot of medical intervention in order for me to get pregnant. Pregnancy for me was only the beginning of my journey and my struggles into parenthood. We tried to keep our eyes on the prize of holding a baby in our arms, no matter what path we took to get there. We kept trying as hard as we could until we could change from being just a couple of people into parents, the title we so desperately strived for.

Along the way, while trying to gain strength, I gained friends who shared their parallel stories with me about trying to start their own families. I learned that I was very much not alone and that it helped us all significantly to be able to share our journeys with one another. What you are about to read is a series of stories that moved me, comforted me, and inspired me—stories of my friends. My hope in sharing them is that it might move, comfort, and inspire you too.

Chapter One

Stefanie

S tefanie met Sydney at a party where friends set them up to meet.

Stefanie was just beginning to see herself as a gay woman: she'd had boyfriends before, but she also found herself attracted to women. She thought maybe she was bisexual; since she felt a certain pressure to pick a side, she did.

Stefanie was open to meeting a new woman at this party, but Sydney, on the other hand, was hesitant since she had only just come out of a nine-year relationship. She had moved to Washington State with her, only to come back to Philly when the seams holding their relationship together ripped apart.

Stefanie was skeptical about getting too involved with someone right out of something so serious, but once she and Sydney started talking that night, they had a hard time stopping. Their conversation started with the usual "Where are you from?" and "What do you do?" Very quickly though they each got the feeling like everything else in the room got blurry and the vision for each other sharpened. Stefanie looked at every detail of Syd, not only what she looked like but also the intensity of her focus when she was speaking. She wanted to dive in for more. Syd stared right back at Stefanie, and was taken aback by her brightness, not only because she was smart but because there was a levity to her that put Syd at ease. They talked so long that they didn't realize the party was ending around them. They ended up at a nearby bar just to stretch out their time together a bit more.

Sydney and Stefanie dated, then they committed to each other, and soon afterward, they moved in together. Syd was matter-of-fact, confident, and competent in getting anything done that needed to be accomplished. She was straightforward, and Stefanie appreciated that quality in Syd. Sydney's appearance almost mimicked her personality: she had straight, short dark hair cleanly cut just above her shoulders and deep brown eyes that looked at everyone seriously until someone earned a smile. Once those eyes were smiling, her whole face would join in and could warm a whole room.

From the beginning, Stefanie made Syd smile. Stefanie's lightness came through instantly to anyone who met her. She had a great sense of humor and the ability to accept life as it was handed to her. She could spin the hardest times into something comical. Stefanie's eyes were a clear light blue that invited Syd to jump into them. Together, they laughed a lot—being together was easy in a way that neither had felt with anyone else. It was clear to them early on that they wanted to spend their lives together.

One night, while lying next to each other, they started talking about the future and what they wanted. "Just so you know, if you ever want to have kids, I can't carry a baby, so you would have to," Stefanie said.

"I don't want to be pregnant. I could be talked into being a parent, but I don't want to actually bear a kid," Syd said. Syd didn't have the longing to be pregnant that some women have. She wanted the child, but the nine months to get there was the unsure part.

"We'll have to figure out something else, I guess. It is physically impossible for me," Stefanie said.

Stefanie was born with a rare congenital disorder known as MRKH Syndrome that only affects about one in every four to five thousand females at birth. It stands for Mayer-Rokitansky-Küster-Hauser, named after the doctors who discovered the condition. Women who have MRKH have normally functioning ovaries but no reproductive organs. When all of Stefanie's friends were getting their periods at thirteen, fourteen, and fifteen, hers never came. When she was sixteen, her mother took her in to see her doctor, and they discovered that Stefanie didn't have a uterus. She would never get a period. She would never have to deal with what other women have to deal with monthly. She could never carry a baby.

From the time Stefanie learned she couldn't have a baby, she remembers accepting the news indifferently. She never dreamed of being a mother. She didn't spend summers being a camp counselor. She had never even babysat for other people's kids; when she learned she couldn't have kids when she was still a kid herself, she accepted the news for what it was. She had a niece who she spent time with and, although she loved hanging out with her, she had no interest in changing her diapers.

When Stefanie and Syd talked about kids, they weren't positive if this was something they wanted to take on. When Syd's friend Brian told them he would help them have kids by being a sperm donor, Syd and Stefanie politely declined. They didn't feel compelled enough to decide.

A few months later, when Syd, who was an executive recruiter, had to work out of New York for a month, they decided it would be fun if Stefanie came along. They lived in Philadelphia and loved New York, but Stefanie typically only went into the city for a day here and there, otherwise working remotely as a freelance copy editor.

Syd's friend Brian lived in Manhattan, and his boyfriend happened to be working out-of-town for most of the time that Syd and Stefanie lived near New York. In his boyfriend's absence, Brian invited them to come to stay with him for a week, and while Syd worked long hours during the day, Brian and Stefanie got to know each other. They listened to great music, ran around the city discovering parts neither had seen before, and ate at impeccable, delicious restaurants.

Brian was ridiculously smart: he'd developed software programs before that was even a thing. Stefanie couldn't understand his job even after he explained it a few times. Brian also seemed to know something about *everything*—there was no topic he wasn't informed on, providing them with endless conversation. Brian was the kind of guy that straight women wished wasn't gay. He was handsome, sharp, and super nice: Stefanie could see why he was one of Syd's closest friends.

After spending time with Brian, Stefanie started to reconsider having a child. If she could have a child that was a mix of Brian and Syd, then that baby would potentially have a winning combination of great genes. She didn't know if she could produce any eggs to contribute to the equation, but she was compelled to pursue all of the possible ways to have a baby.

"Syd, I know this might not be the ideal time to put this on your radar, with how intense your work load has been this week, but I think maybe we should reconsider the baby idea. I think I want one." Stefanie said. Syd was taken aback by how a wave of excitement rose in her stomach while Stefanie talked about a baby. She was overwhelmed by her nervous anticipation and enthusiasm. Syd was speechless though and Stefanie kept talking until it reassured her concerns. Together they agreed to give it a try. One try.

Brian had extended the first offer, so Stefanie hoped he would still be interested. It was quite some time after his original offer, what if he had changed his mind? Earlier that month at the start of their visit to New York, Brian had told them that another couple had asked him to help them, and he had turned them down— in his heart he didn't feel that they would make good parents. Stefanie and Syd decided to approach him and ask again.

"Just tell me when and where to be," Brian responded.

After a few months of research to find out what would work best for everyone time wise and to process the idea of actually trying to have a baby together, Stefanie and Syd went to a fertility specialist. They decided to increase their chances of fertility by having the specialist retrieve eggs from both Stefanie and Sydney. Both women were in their mid-to-late thirties, and, with Stefanie's reproductive system already compromised, they weren't sure how much luck they would have on their side.

After injecting themselves with hormones, Stefanie and Syd followed the exact protocol as their doctor instructed them—but despite their efforts, Sydney produced only five eggs, and Stefanie only three. Most women are able to produce between ten and twenty eggs from one treatment. Stefanie and Syd produced a total of eight together; the odds were stacked against them.

Fertility treatments are expensive. Legal fees are expensive. The medications needed for the treatments were an additional cost. Considering the various challenges, Stefanie and Syd had a long discussion before trying to create embryos from any of these eight eggs, on the very likely possibility that this might not happen for them. They decided that no matter the outcome, this would be their only attempt.

Next, Syd and Stefanie reached out to Brian to begin the legal paperwork needed for him to become their donor. They learned that, in addition to the hefty fee the lawyer would get for drawing up the paperwork, they also needed to provide proof of a financial exchange with Brian. He did not want money from them and considered this all a gift. Stefanie and Syd paid him one dollar and bought him a pint of ice cream, as documented evidence the lawyer needed, to show that Brian was paid.

Once all the puzzle pieces were in place, Stefanie and Syd learned that, from these eight eggs, about eighty percent would make it through the first phase of the process. Their doctors spoke of *attrition,* so they went home to Google it. Attrition meant the rate at which the viable eggs taper off once they are in the lab and growing: only mature eggs will fertilize and, since the rate of growth for eggs happens at different paces, there is significant variation in viability.

"At our geriatric age of close to forty, surely our eggs are nice and mature as well." Stefanie joked, but it seemed to be a requirement for practically all their fertility doctors to have zero sense of humor. Syd smirked and gave Stefanie a leg squeeze of acknowledgment as they tried to follow the math lesson they were being given. They learned the next phase of attrition was called the blastocyst phase: the embryos that survive the whole process, and that have been left to grow in the lab undisturbed for five days are the ones with the best potential to implant. This meant that, if they started with eight and then accounted for the eighty percent, then they maybe had six...and after the first phase, only thirty to fifty percent reached attrition, so they would get three chances at best.

Stefanie and Syd ended up with two embryos. They decided to increase their odds and implant both—if they had twins, then the whole "nuclear family" would be decided for them, even though they still weren't sure they wanted more than one child.

On the day of the procedure, Stefanie got up and made Syd breakfast. "If I could, I would, but I can't, so..." Stefanie said playfully. She could see Syd was nervous.

Syd ate a few bites of food, mostly because she didn't want to turn down Stefanie's kind gesture, but she wasn't hungry. "Babe, said Stefanie, "one time, and then we don't have to ever try this again. If it doesn't work, we will book airline tickets to travel somewhere far, far away. Deal?"

"Deal—and I also get to pick what we watch tonight," said Syd.

Later that day, Stefanie and Syd held hands as the two embryos were transferred into Syd's uterus. When the doctor left the room after the procedure, they squeezed each other's hands with nervous excitement. They knew better than to get too attached to the idea that the procedure could work, but they were both more hopeful than they let on to be.

The waiting was brutal, so they both did the best they could to stay busy and distracted. They went on a lot of walks, watched a lot more television, and took up an elaborate new cooking hobby. Ten days later Syd took a home pregnancy test by peeing on a stick, and after a few very long minutes, it showed up with two lines meaning that indicated pregnancy. They had to wait to find out for sure though at their OB's office. Four days later, a blood test revealed that Syd was indeed pregnant. They scheduled another exam for two weeks later to check her blood hormone levels.

Both Syd and Stefanie were happy with the news, but they kept it to themselves until they had more information. At this second appointment, the doctor was so serious again when he delivered any news to them. "This is the first step—and good news, a transfer was successful, but now we need to see how it goes from here." Syd and Stefanie nodded along with him while he spoke but looked for an indication that they could smile. They weren't sure what emotional response they were supposed to have whenever he delivered them information. Again they waited for him to leave the room and then their eyes widened. They both pursed their mouths shut with their lips curled inward like puppets. They wanted to scream or laugh—but given where they were and the tone of the office, they whisper-shouted their excitement instead.

"Holy shit, Syd! You are *pregnant*!" Stefanie said as if she was telling a secret

"That's what he said, right? Pretty amazing that it actually worked!" Syd whispered back.

They went home and waited another two weeks before they returned for the first ultrasound. During those two weeks, a full range of emotions passed between Stefanie and Syd. They had moments of being terrified of the idea of becoming parents, that they might have lost their freedom forever. What if they weren't cut out for this at all? What if Syd hated being pregnant? What if she messed up and ate all the wrong foods—or worse, couldn't eat at all? Then they felt the excitement of having a child. They wondered about who this little person would be, and what they might look like. They joked about what music to play the baby first, what books to read to the baby, and who would take the first night shift or change the first diaper.

At their first ultrasound appointment, Syd and Stefanie waited in the examination room for the doctor to come in. Syd sat on the edge of the exam table wearing the flimsy paper gown.

"You know how I told you if I could, I would trade places with you?" Stefanie said. "I think I take it back. I am comfortable over here, fully dressed and warm."

"If you are trying to make me feel better, it's not really working," said Syd.

"I'm not. I'm just making an observation," replied Stefanie.

They waited together, trying to ease the tension in the room. When the doctor came in, he asked Syd how she was feeling and a couple more matter-of-fact, obligatory questions.

"Okay, let's take a look, shall we?" He said it more like a statement than a question. He explained how the ultrasound, in the beginning, was done with a vaginal wand and Syd nodded, shooting Stefanie a dirty look.

Once he began explaining what he saw on the monitor, the tone in the room turned. It grew quiet as he explained that he saw the sac where the beginning of the pregnancy had started but stopped developing. He called it a "blighted ovum" and said that it appeared that no embryo was growing. For the first time since they had begun working together, the doctor showed a tiny hint of emotion.

"This might result in a miscarriage on its own," he said, "and after a few weeks, if it doesn't, we can do a D&C here in the office. Before we do anything, though, I would like to wait a week and see you again. It can be hard to see what is happening this early on, and although it is not likely, there could be some new development in the next few days." He gave them the impression to come back expecting the worst. He sent them home for more waiting, but they went home to mourn.

They spent the week planning how they would move forward. They both admitted being more disappointed than they expected. They hadn't told anyone, so they didn't have anyone to call to share the sad news with. They thought about the trip they had promised each other they would plan, but neither of them felt very inspired. Each of them tried, both separately and together, to distract themselves, but this time nothing worked. They couldn't escape their sadness.

The night before the next ultrasound appointment, Syd and Stefanie made a special dinner to honor the baby that didn't come to be. If they weren't going to have a baby, they could at least order in the expensive sushi they both loved. They shared a bottle of sake and toasted their child-free future. Over dessert, they talked about how to begin the rest of their lives on this second-choice path. They came up short on ideas, so they researched books and found one called *Choosing To Be Child Free*—even though the title implied they had made that choice on their own. They each shared a few words to Syd's belly and the baby that wouldn't come to be. They thanked the baby for making them mamas even for that short little window of time.

At the appointment the next day, an ultrasound technician met them in the room: their regular doctor had to be with another patient. Although this woman didn't know them or their situation outside of what their paperwork said, Syd and Stefanie welcomed having a stranger with them. They were quiet and subdued as the woman went through the routine questions and niceties.

"We kind of have a feeling we aren't getting great news today," admitted Stefanie, while Syd's eyes darted around the room avoiding any other person's eyes. She didn't like crying in public, but she was struggling to keep her eyes dry as Stefanie talked. Stefanie's way of keeping it together was to keep talking—even though the technician had no more medical advice or information for them.

After what felt like an hour of staring at the medical jars, sink, and phone buttons, Syd couldn't wait any longer. "So do you do the ultrasound and then report the results back to the doctor?" she asked as nicely as she could muster, hoping to get this all over with. After all, she was the one sitting with a paper gown exposed both physically and emotionally.

"Let's take a look," said the technician, facing Syd and acknowledging her nervousness. This wasn't this woman's first rodeo; the way she took control of the room at that moment made Syd so relieved that they weren't meeting with their regular doctor.

"Hips just a bit closer to the end of the table—this will feel a little cold at first." The technician explained everything as she did it, which helped Syd get out of her head and into what was happening.

After that, "I'm sorry" were the first words that the technician said. Both Syd and Stefanie knew she kept speaking, but they stuck on those two words, processing that the end of their idea to have a baby had arrived. They both stared at the monitor and saw the sac and dark grey shadow of what represented the start and end of their family.

"Hang on for one moment," the tech said as she stared at the screen. She slowly rotated the wand while looking intently at the monitor, enough so that Syd felt the uncomfortable pressure. Suddenly a completely different view appeared on the screen: what had before looked still now had movement and sound.

The tech smiled and pointed to the sac. "This is your baby, and that sound is the heart beating," she said. The shock made both Stefanie and Syd speechless as the mood in the room transformed. Syd covered her mouth because her jaw dropped so much. She let herself cry, this time full of joy. She hadn't let herself admit how much she also wanted a baby until she realized she might not ever have one. The relief softened the fists she had been clenching.

Stefanie froze as she watched the movement of the tiny heart beating. She looked over at Syd and laughed, wrapping her arms around Syd and kissing her. Stefanie couldn't stop looking back at the monitor as if to keep confirming that this was all real.

"Wait, I am just trying to put this all together," Syd said. What was it we saw first that made it seem like we weren't pregnant?"

"You had two embryos implanted," the tech said. "The first one we were looking at was the one that didn't take, but the second one is this one here." Stefanie and Syd had only been shown one embryo during the first ultrasound, so they'd assumed that only one ever implanted.

As they processed the good news, the technician left them in the room to dress and leave. They went home that day in a much lighter mood than when they came in. With Brian's help, the help of science, and the eventful path that they were on Syd and Stefanie would become the parents they had hoped to be.

They went home that night and celebrated once again, but not before exchanging the book they purchased about being child-free for a parenting handbook.

Chapter Two

Keisha

After giving birth to her baby girl, Keisha held her baby in her arms and cried. She was so elated to have heard a healthy cry and to have her baby safely handed to her so quickly. This moment was what Keisha had hoped for four years before when she and her husband Chris decided to start a family.

Before her children were born, Keisha had a nonchalant attitude about becoming pregnant and giving birth. At the time she was thirty-one years old, ready for what felt like the obvious next step in their life. She'd made a career change after being a flight attendant for almost twelve years: she had traveled the world, made a good living, and now, she was ready for something new.

Keisha got a job as an executive assistant to Charles—the CEO of Glow, a new makeup line. He was a great boss: kind, respectful, and appreciative of Keisha. Charles, who was in his sixties, had started many companies over the years and wasn't flustered by the day-to-day issues that were stressful to his employees. His attitude and approach were a great match for Keisha. She was great at getting tasks checked off her list, was a hard worker, and did her job well, but didn't get caught up in the drama that swarmed around the office.

After work, she took the train home to Chris. Some nights, they met in the city for dinner, taking the train back to New Jersey together. Those were her favorite nights—the nights their timing worked out just right. Those nights made her feel like the workday ended early and they got to go on a surprise date.

Chris worked in business development on the Upper East Side, and his company provided them both with an extensive health insurance policy. Keisha found an in-network OB and made an appointment, in preparation for getting pregnant. Like every decision Keisha made, she chose her doctor based on multiple factors: she wanted a woman, she wanted someone located close to both Chris's and her office, and she wanted someone with experience practicing medicine.

At her first appointment, Keisha explained that she was ready to start trying to get pregnant and wanted to meet before to see if there were any special vitamins she should take, or if she should eat anything specific that might help her body prepare for pregnancy.

"There are a few things you should take," the doctor told her, "but one step at a time. Get pregnant first and then you can take prenatal vitamins and folic acid. As for what you eat, if it is healthy and balanced, then you should be fine."

Her doctor was nice enough, for a doctor, Keisha thought. She was a bit matter-of-fact and direct. If it was anyone else, Keisha would have categorized her as a bit cold, but many doctors have distant bedside manners. Keisha wrote off her concerns and reminded herself that this woman was very experienced. On the way home on the train later that day, Keisha replayed her appointment in her mind. She told herself that it was okay if she didn't love her new doctor. The doctor didn't need to be her best friend—she just needed to be a good doctor, and based on all of the reviews she read, they indicated that she was.

After a few months of trying, Keisha got a positive pregnancy test. She had gotten a pack of two tests at the drugstore, and to make sure the first positive wasn't a mistake, she took both. Both tests had two pink lines. She read the back of the box and confirmed that two lines meant pregnant.

Shocked, she wanted Chris to experience the same surprise—so she washed one of the sticks and wrapped the test in a rectangular gift box, tying a ribbon around it. Chris was dressed for work and getting his coffee ready when Keisha sat down at the table to join him for a quick breakfast. As he sat down with his cup, she slid the box over to him.

"What's this, baby? Chris asked.

"Just a little something I threw together. Open it," said Keisha.

Chris smiled as he pulled the ribbon to untie the bow. He opened the box and looked down at the white plastic stick with two pink lines and furrowed his brow. He looked confused, then concerned, and then hopeful. Keisha, entertained, watched him trying to figure out exactly what the stick meant.

"Does this mean what I think it means? Are we having a baby?" Chris asked.

Keisha nodded yes and smiled. Chris cheered so loudly that Keisha was afraid the neighbors might get worried. He couldn't wipe the smile off his face the whole day. They took the train into the city for work, grabbing each other's hands, laughing together, and reminding each other that they were going to have a baby.

"You are going to be this baby's daddy, Chris. Can you believe that?" Keisha asked.

"I better be this baby's daddy." Chris joked. She elbowed him and then rested her head on his shoulder to lose herself in her daydreams. Neither one could make it through their workday without calling each other every few hours, pinching each other that they were actually going to have a baby. Keisha smiled to herself every time she thought of her little secret growing inside her. She knew that, as early on as she was in the pregnancy, miscarriage was a possibility—but she allowed herself the time to fantasize about becoming a mother.

At Keisha's next doctor appointment, she and Chris went together. When she told the doctor that she got a positive pregnancy test, she had hoped the doctor would have shown a bit more emotion—or had at least more of a reaction than she did. She was once again very matter-of-fact. Keisha was glad Chris was with her, so he could see why Keisha was conflicted about her personality. The doctor ordered a blood test to confirm the pregnancy by checking the hormone levels. When the doctor asked them if they had any more questions, Keisha took out a little piece of paper. She read off the first question and looked up to see the doctor's response.

"Just go ahead and read them all to me, and I will answer afterward." was the doctor's response.

As Keisha read off each question, she squeezed Chris's hand. She had never been pregnant before, so she didn't know what a doctor-patient relationship was supposed to be like, but she had hoped for more than this woman was giving her. When she was done reading the questions, she looked up once again for the doctor's response.

"Let's see what comes back from the blood test results. Go ahead and start taking your vitamins and folic acid, and let's take everything else from there," the doctor said.

"Um, ok. One last question. If all goes well, when will be the first ultrasound?" Keisha asked.

"At the next appointment, which will be in three weeks," the doctor said as she collected her chart and headed towards the door.

"Thank you. Nice meeting you," Chris said.

Keisha changed into her clothes and stayed quiet until they were out of the building. She looked at Chris to see what he thought. She'd felt brushed aside in the appointment—she couldn't even get one of her questions answered. Sure, she could look them up online, but she wanted to hear answers from her doctor.

Chris agreed that the woman was not extremely friendly, but figured it was par for the course since a lot of doctors are like that—especially a lot of white doctors. He reassured Keisha that she was probably going to be fine and that maybe the doctor-patient relationship would get better in time. Keisha wondered if maybe doctors don't warm up until pregnancies look more viable. Maybe the doctor's bedside manner was by design.

For the first trimester, pregnancy was kind to Keisha. She didn't have morning sickness, she had that famous pregnancy glow, and her belly grew straight out in front in the most adorable way. When she went to work, Charles went out of his way to make sure Keisha was feeling okay—he even told her she could work from home if it helped and gave her the option to come back part-time after her maternity leave was done. He joked that he was getting an assistant and a half for the price of one. Keisha was grateful for the way he looked out for her, and for having the kind of job that she could manage while pregnant. She was glad she made the choice to stop traveling when she did.

Working in the city and commuting each day worked well for Keisha for the first half of her pregnancy. Once she reached the second half, her legs started to swell, making it harder and harder to walk from the train station to the office. She also found herself constantly thirsty and took to sucking on a huge cup of ice that she kept at her desk. She noticed she kept going through cup after cup not feeling like she was getting quenched. Growing concerned, Keisha called her doctor to tell her about her symptoms. She left a message with the receptionist and, the next day, the receptionist called her back, telling her that the doctor said that she was experiencing normal symptoms of pregnancy.

Keisha felt parched all the time. She didn't go anywhere without several big bottles of water, for fear of getting stuck without hydration. Keisha looked up what it could mean to be so thirsty, and saw online that it could be a sign of gestational diabetes. It also said that tests for gestational diabetes are given between twenty-four and twenty-eight weeks. She wasn't tested for gestational diabetes until twenty-nine weeks and waited two weeks for the results.

At thirty-one weeks into her pregnancy, Keisha was diagnosed with gestational diabetes. For the first time, she saw her doctor take action to make sure that Keisha's condition was monitored. Keisha was advised to cut out sugar, fruits, bread, and starchy foods. She obliged and completely changed her diet, doing everything she could to make sure that she and the baby would be okay. She researched healthy snack options and started eating more nuts, vegetables, and legumes. She started to feel better—but when she went to her next appointment, it seemed her blood sugar levels hadn't lowered enough to stay diet-controlled, so she was put on medication to stabilize them.

Chris enjoyed the challenge of finding culinary concoctions that were low in sugars but high in flavor and fats. In solidarity with Keisha, he changed his diet to match hers, even when they weren't eating meals together. Chris lost five pounds and looked great—but Keisha felt she was not only growing bigger and bigger but also moving slower and slower.

To treat her diabetes, Keisha found an online support group for women with gestational diabetes where people traded stories, recipes, and support. Her levels stabilized, and she became able to manage her sugars quite well. She found she actually enjoyed eggs and avocado for breakfast. She was getting the hang of the new diet and didn't feel as thirsty all the time.

Keisha had been so focused on getting her and the baby healthy that she hadn't had time to focus on a birthing plan. She and Chris didn't have it in them to go to a class so instead, they took a course online at home. They practiced breathing exercises and came up with a birthing wish list that included wanting to labor naturally as long as possible before being given medications. Keisha packed a hospital bag to have ready when she needed it and took extra care in washing and folding the tiniest little onesie to bring her baby home in.

At thirty-six weeks, Keisha had planned to finish her last few weeks of work and then take some time off before giving birth. It wasn't uncommon for first babies to be a bit late, so she hoped this would guarantee her some time to rest and to prepare—but her baby had other plans. The Tuesday morning of her last week of work, Keisha was getting ready when her water broke.

"Chris!" she shrieked. Chris came running into the room and saw fluid drenching his wife's pants and a puddle on the floor.

"This is way early, right?" He asked. Keisha nodded and pointed to her cell phone. It was a few feet away from her, but she was afraid to move.

She called the doctor's office and was instructed to make her way to the hospital. As she cleaned herself up, she had Chris call her office and their family to let them know they were in labor. Charles immediately called back Keisha's phone and Chris answered.

"Chris, please tell Keisha not to worry about anything at work. We have got everything covered and all she needs to do is go have a baby," said Charles. When Chris relayed this message to Keisha, she started to cry. She knew she was lucky to have a boss who was so understanding, especially since she was leaving work over two weeks before she had planned.

Keisha's labor was progressing, and she and Chris were able to manage it together quite well. He guided her through breathing during her contractions and he tracked her contractions diligently. They took a cab to the hospital. When there was traffic going through the Lincoln Tunnel, Keisha panicked, afraid that they would get stuck rubbernecking and she would become one of the women she'd heard stories about who gave birth in the back of the car. She closed her eyes and didn't open them until the cab was out of the tunnel.

Once Keisha was checked into a delivery room, nurses examined Keisha and found that she was six centimeters dilated. This news was a comfort to her: her body was doing what it needed to do, and she took pride in achieving six whole centimeters already.

The doctor arrived, checked Keisha's updated chart, and walked up to Keisha and Chris.

"So, this is earlier than we expected," she said.

Instead of the doctor's comment feeling tongue-in-cheek, Chris sensed that she was inconvenienced by Keisha's early labor. He knew better than to say anything, though. Their priority was getting their baby out, not teaching the doctor the ABCs of basic good manners. He had felt this sensation before, many times, as an African-American man—the dismissive looks and diminished attentiveness that is given to others in the same room. He took a deep breath and let it go. He wasn't going to fix a broken system, especially not the day he was going to become a father. He shifted his focus to Keisha and made sure he did what he could to protect her.

Both Keisha and the baby were doing well. She had gotten an epidural and was able to rest a bit. As her contractions grew closer and closer together, the doctor examined her cervix. She said it was thinning more on one side than the other, but that Keisha should be safe to start pushing.

After a few pushes, the baby's head was out. Chris cheered Keisha on and let her know how well she was doing.

"I see our baby, Keisha. You have got this. I see hair, eyes, a nose, a mouth—we made a little person, babe," Chris said as he practically jumped up and down.

As Keisha bore down to push the next few times, the baby didn't move. Suddenly, her monitors started beeping; her bedside care grew from just her doctor to what felt like five more surrounding her, pressing on her belly. In the shuffle, Keisha lost sight of Chris. She started to panic and wanted to ask what was happening, but she couldn't find the words or the strength to ask. She looked up and found one doctor holding her leg, another starting to cut to help get the baby out, and another pulling at the baby, all while her doctor supervised and said nothing.

Finally, the doctor who was pushing down on her belly told Keisha that the baby was stuck against her pelvis—they were doing everything they could to get the baby out safely. Keisha pursed her lips together, trying not to cry out. She knew that she needed to keep breathing. She remembered a line from one of her pregnancy books: in order to keep the body's muscles relaxed during birth, you have to also keep your facial muscles relaxed. Whatever the facial muscles do, the book said, so do the vaginal muscles. Keisha fought hard against furrowing her brow. She put her head back against the bed and prayed. She closed her eyes and tried to drown out the lights, beeps, and people swarming around her.

"Give us one more big push!" they yelled, and she obliged.

Keisha felt a huge alleviation of pressure, and—despite being numb from the epidural—she felt her legs release from the doctor's arms. Chris rushed over to her, his face wet with tears.

"The baby is out. Looks like a boy, but they are working on him," Chris whispered.

Keisha held her breath, waiting to hear her baby take his. She wanted more than anything to hear her baby cry. She had waited for this moment for the last nine months and had never prepared herself for a birth as traumatic as the one she just had. She lifted her head and saw all the doctors who had surrounded her only a few moments before now huddled around her baby, pressing over and over on his chest to administer CPR.

After three minutes—which felt like three hours to Keisha—the baby finally began to breathe and the doctors were able to stabilize him. They rushed him to the NICU for tests, and Chris followed the baby. Keisha finally exhaled. One of the doctors came in to speak with her, and he explained that the shoulder of the baby was too big and that he got stuck, which sent him into distress. He also explained that her gestational diabetes was likely the reason why the baby was so big and that she should have been treated earlier for the condition. He didn't point fingers—but he didn't have to. Keisha's instincts were right all along. She never felt cared for by her doctor, and now she understood that her traumatic birth could have been avoided if she had been shown a bit more respect. Keisha didn't doubt that, if her skin or Chris's skin were lighter, their baby might not have ended up in the NICU.

By the time Keisha was strong enough to visit her newborn son, he was hooked up to tubes: heart rate and blood pressure monitors were stuck on his chest, and both of his wrists were wrapped with IV ports for medication. His beautiful head was covered with medical tape to secure the probes that checked his brain activity. He had an oxygen tube in his tiny nose and a feeding tube threaded through the remainder of his umbilical cord. Faces of people came in, one after another, to check on him. Keisha watched as her baby—which was hers, that she waited so long for—was cared for by other people's hands. While she was grateful that her son was finally getting the high-quality medical care that they both should have received all along, she was devastated that he had been handled by so many others before she even had a chance to hold him in her arms.

Chris wrapped his arms around Keisha, and together they stared at their baby. It was terrifying waiting to see if he would be healthy, so they mapped out all of the perfect parts of his body. The little bit of hair on his head, his ears, nose, his rosebud lips. His ten fingers and ten toes. His strong kicking legs.

"We should give this guy a name. Don't you think?" Chris asked.

"Josiah," Keisha said, without hesitation. It was a name at the top of their list. "Since it means God will save, I am really hoping he will live up to that name right about now."

"Fair enough. Josiah it is. It suits him....right, Josiah?" Chris explored the sound of his son's name rolling off his tongue.

For two weeks, Josiah stayed in the hospital to be monitored. He went home with a weaker shoulder on one side but otherwise completely healthy. Keisha and Chris thought that he might have more health issues, but his care team said his shoulder was either going to heal on its own or—more likely—he would need some physical therapy to help him gain strength as he got older.

Once the new family walked into their house after being away for so long, Keisha finally held Josiah on her own without all the chaos of the hospital around her. She kissed his head and thanked God for keeping him safe, healthy, and alive.

Keisha and Chris learned to become parents and Josiah learned how much he was loved—but whenever they thought about having another baby, the trauma of their start echoed loudly. They wanted a sibling for Josiah, but it would take them three years of recovery to even consider trying again.

When they did decide to try again, they made the decision to have a midwife work with them. Keisha wanted to be with people who looked like her and had her best interests at heart. They found midwives who were part of a group that advocates for women of color. The three women who owned the company all had experienced racism in their own maternal care and wanted to offer an option for women where they would feel heard, seen, and respected.

When Keisha had her first visit with the midwives, she asked questions—and right away, based on their caring response, she felt she was in the right hands. When she and Chris had questions for her last doctor, they were made to feel like they were aggressive or confrontational just for asking. With her midwife, Keisha felt held. She felt that they cared for her and she had a team around her that she could trust.

Unlike her last pregnancy, this time Keisha was given the test for diabetes much earlier on in the twenty-fourth week. Together with her team of midwives, they planned a healthy diet for Keisha to follow and fortunately, all the efforts were not in vain. Her blood test came back and her sugar levels were normal and healthy. When Keisha started to have contractions, she panicked a little. She tried to remember if she had packed a bag for the hospital—and then she remembered that she wasn't going to the hospital this time. That thought alone relaxed her so much. With Chris by her side, they tracked the time between each contraction. She was calm enough to call the midwife and let her know her status.

When it was time to begin delivery, the midwife came over—as well as both Keisha and Chris's mothers, who took turns caring for Josiah. Having them there meant to Keisha that everyone in the world who she loved the most was surrounding her and protecting her.

The midwives helped Chris fill an inflatable birthing pool that Keisha rented per the midwives' advice. It was big enough for her to move around in, and the sides were soft enough that she could lean on it. She felt at ease in the little pool.

The water was warm, and she was able to relax completely in between her contractions. When she felt the pressure and urge to push, the midwife was right by her side, reminding her what to do. The room was so peaceful, the lights comforting and the sounds familiar. It was so opposite to her last birthing experience.

Keisha closed her eyes on her next contraction and listened to the midwife's calming voice. She followed her cues and pushed when she felt like she needed to. By her side, Chris encouraged her gently, telling her how well she was doing. She took another push.

"Reach down and feel your baby," the midwife told her. Keisha pushed one more time, then reached for the baby and placed the newborn on her chest. The first thing Keisha heard was the sound of her daughter's cry—and then the sound of her own, as her healthy baby stayed on her body.

Her baby girl came into the world without trauma. Chris wrapped his arms around Keisha and their daughter. "This is different," he said smiling as they both took in the peacefulness in the room. Keisha took a long deep breath, looked down at her baby girl, and said "Yup, she is pretty beautiful." They felt relaxed and at ease knowing their family was complete, at home, and healthy.

Chapter Three

Jillian

J illian knew she would end up living in the city: you either stay on Long Island your whole life, or you escape. Jillian wanted to follow her brother to Penn State and then move back to NY to live in Manhattan. Her plan was proceeding on schedule when she moved into an apartment with her friend Claire: they both had jobs waiting tables while they looked for acting and dance work. She got to do a commercial, and she shot an episode of *Law and Order*. She made enough money to pay her rent between the restaurant and her gigs.

One night, when she and Claire were walking home together from grabbing dinner at their regular spot DoJo's, Jillian turned to Claire and asked "Can you believe we both live here? That we said this is what we wanted, and here we are?" Claire smiled in agreement. They danced home that night proudly.

About a year after being in Manhattan, Jillian got a part in an Off-Broadway play. The job was with a theatre company, and she enjoyed working with a group of talented actors who were all around her age. When she wasn't working, she was hanging out with the company members. There were always drinks or dinner after rehearsal, and she looked forward to these nights. Many of the members were hooking up, and Jillian had a few flings of her own. It was all light and fun—until the night she met Noah.

Noah was a part of the company but had been out of town working on a short when Jillian was first hired. She had heard his name mentioned, but that night was the first time she met him. After they were introduced, they returned to their previous conversations with others—but every time Jillian looked over at Noah, he seemed to be looking back. Whenever they would catch each other's eyes, they would both smile and try to look away again. This went on for what felt like an hour to Jillian but was probably more like ten minutes. She was talking to a friend when she looked up and saw Noah. He pulled up a chair to join them, and the three of them talked until most of their other friends were starting to leave. She and her friend had planned on walking back home together, so Jillian wasn't able to talk to Noah alone that night. They said goodbye, and Jillian went to bed that night thinking about Noah.

When Jillian got home from her shift at the restaurant the next day, a message from Noah waited for her on her answering machine. He said he really enjoyed meeting her and wanted to know if she would like to go out with him sometime soon. She listened to the message, then replayed it four more times before she realized she hadn't even taken her coat off. She felt an unfamiliar chill run down her spine, and a flip of excitement rose from the bottom of her stomach. Jillian met Noah the next free night she had, and from that night on they were rarely apart. The air tasted sweet. The colors looked more vibrant. The city noise blended together playing a soundtrack for the two of them.

Noah worked as an actor and tended bar to pay his bills. He seemed to know everyone in New York, and seemingly everywhere he and Jillian went, they would run into someone Noah knew. He was excited to introduce her to people and was always looking for ways to help her get acting work. They were supportive of each other's successes. Noah made professional introductions; together, they made plans on how to move forward in both of their careers.

Jillian had never met anyone so sweet, and she sank into Noah's kindness. Jillian had been in a few relationships with a few guys that turned out to be awful. As things got more serious with Noah, she went to therapy to make sure she didn't repeat the mistakes of her past. She felt so elated, but also wanted to make sure she had her feet on the ground. Even though it was hard since she felt like she was floating most of the time. They were in love with each other and in love with being in love. The feeling never faded, either. For the next two years, whenever they started kissing, they had a hard time stopping.

Trying to work as an actor and create a life in New York is not easy—trying to do anything in New York is not easy, but being an artist is especially challenging. Jillian didn't mind the challenge, though. Noah was so passionate, so smitten with her, and she loved being his girlfriend.

One afternoon when they both had a day off to spend together, they were walking through Central Park. As they both walked closer to the carousel, Noah faced Jillian, and in his hands were two little red tickets. "Want to go for a ride?" He asked as he gestured toward the carousel.

"On the merry-go-round?" She asked, smiling. He looked her back in the eyes, and then without losing eye contact leaned down on one knee.

"And in life. Jillian, will you marry me?" When Noah asked her to marry him, she was so surprised and so happy.

Jillian said yes, and they began to plan their wedding at a beautiful rustic barn about two hours outside the city. Her bridesmaids were a mix of her closest friends from Long Island, her college friends, and her new friends from living in the city. They helped Jillian find the perfect wedding dress, and together, they had a dressmaker begin making dresses for all of them.

Her parents liked Noah but weren't sure they liked him for Jillian. He hadn't gone to college, didn't have a steady job, and wasn't quite grown enough to be marrying their daughter, they felt. He was an actor without any backup plan should his career not take off. He had no other goals, plans, or ideas other than being an actor and living in New York. When her parents tried to ask him about the future they could tell he was trying hard to change the subject.

The invitations were out and RSVPs were arriving, as well as wedding gifts. The wedding date grew closer—and problems in their relationship started to appear more clearly to Jillian. One day, when Jillian was out choosing between caterers, an electrician was supposed to come to their apartment. Jillian asked Noah if he could deal with it while she was out, and his response surprised her. He asked her what he needed to do—he didn't know what to say, or how to handle such a small task.

Jillian had a few other moments like these with Noah where she took pause. She felt dread bubbling in her gut and wondered: if she married Noah, would he eventually grow up? Would he learn over time how to take care of himself? Would he ever make enough money to not live rent-to-rent? She pushed down her worries and chalked them up to nerves before the wedding.

As the wedding got closer, Jillian started having trouble sleeping. She was losing weight because she couldn't eat. She had finally met a kindhearted man who loved her and had broken her pattern of finding men who didn't value or respect her—so why was her gut screaming louder with each passing day? She wished she could stop time for long enough to think. She wanted to catch her breath and slow everything down.

As Jillian's doubt grew, her mother could see her daughter was not doing well. Seeing Jillian so consumed by ambivalence was impossible for her to ignore. Weeks before the big day, Jillian's mother told her that it was okay to not go through with the wedding. Jillian began to cry as her mother spoke. She felt helpless. She knew she loved Noah—that she was sure of—but she wasn't sure that love was enough of a reason to get married. While she nodded along behind the tears that were flooding her eyes, she didn't share one way or another what she wanted to do about the wedding. She didn't know what to say; she was stuck, confused, and—more than anything—she did not want to hurt Noah.

With each day that passed, Jillian's mother would remind her that she needed to decide if she wanted to get married. Jillian agreed that her relationship with Noah was flawed, but her heart broke imagining calling off her wedding. Jillian's mother interpreted this agreeing as Jillian's decision to cancel the wedding. When Jillian was out the next day, Noah called her mother's home looking for her. Jillian's mother answered the phone, and Noah warmly greeted her. Her response to her daughter's fiancé was an apology.

"I'm so sorry things worked out this way, Noah," she said. Unsure of what was happening, Noah asked Jillian to please call him back right away.

Before the wedding bells could even ring, Jillian and Noah's bell was unrung. There was no way going back now: her mother had initiated the beginning of the end, but Jillian couldn't fight to get the train back on the tracks, because she knew it was broken. Back in the city, just the two of them in their apartment, Jillian and Noah held each other and cried. Noah was shocked, hurt, and devastated.

He pleaded with Jillian to explain what happened. Between sobs, Jillian did her best to explain that she wasn't ready to get married. She assured him that she still loved him, but she just couldn't go through with the wedding. Noah, in his pure compassionate way, stood by Jillian and continued to love her. The bond between them, now significantly melting away, was wearing the thin ice they were already skating on.

Making the big life decision to cancel a wedding had taken a toll, and Jillian's body was shutting down. She had announced to everyone she knew that she found the love of her life and was getting married—she then had to let each of these people know that she was calling it all off...due to what? Cold feet? Had she jumped in too soon? Did she misjudge? Did she owe an explanation at all? Wasn't canceling enough of a message?

Even though Jillian was on the pill, the stress from canceling the wedding was affecting her cycle. Despite all that had weakened between them, Noah and Jillian were still living together and still making love, proving to each other that not all was lost. Trying to walk on shaky legs over all of the eggshells that remained between them, the two of them tried desperately to rebuild their life back as a couple. An ominous, unaddressed air swirled between them whenever they were together.

For the second month in a row, Jillian's cycle was off and her period didn't show up when it was expected. She went to her OB to explain the stress and hopefully be reassured that irregularity was to be expected under the circumstances. Instead, Jillian learned that—two months after calling off her wedding, even while taking birth control—she was pregnant.

On the way home from her doctor's appointment, all Jillian could think was *how did everything get so fucked up?* She unlocked her apartment door and saw that Noah was home. Right away, he saw her face was red and swollen from crying. There was no way she could hold onto the news a second longer. He took in what she was saying silently. Again, they held each other and cried. If Noah had feelings about what Jillian should do next, he didn't say. He knew enough that she was already conflicted about their relationship. It was her body, and she needed to decide what to do.

Jillian told no one that she was pregnant other than Noah. She was already so disappointed that her planned path had crumbled in front of her. She was embarrassed to show anyone else just how shattered she felt. On her own, she decided that she couldn't bring a baby into her mess. She knew that she and Noah weren't doing well together, and she was already afraid of taking care of him—how could she also take care of a baby?

Noah supported her decision and took her to her appointment at the clinic. Jillian had a few friends who'd had an abortion, but she never thought she would be sitting waiting for one. She had always been so careful with birth control—and for this to happen while on the pill proved that so much in her life was slipping out of her grasp.

While having the procedure done, she looked up at the blank ceiling, letting the weight of her head sink heavily into the pad of the table. She tuned out everything going on in her head and in her body. She stared straight into the paint bubbles looking for constellations to connect dot to dot. She wouldn't move until someone told her what to do next.

The same city that Jillian had loved so much was beginning to close in on her. She needed space, and she needed to be on her own. She decided to go to LA for a few months to see if she could piece herself back together, taking her beloved cat Fran with her. She needed distance from Noah, but he couldn't quite distance himself from her. Remaining respectful of what she wished, he asked if he could go to LA as well—but they would stay in two different places. That way they would be apart, but not three thousand miles apart. Since Jillian didn't want to lose him, she agreed.

In LA, they spent a year and a half together but living separately, then breaking up for a few awful months and getting back together again. In the end, it was Noah who put an end to all the back and forth: he just couldn't keep repeating the past. He broke up with Jillian and returned to New York.

Jillian stayed in LA and tried to make a new life for herself. She met her friends for dinners, went to parties, took classes, and acted in more plays—but she wore her sadness like a heavy coat she was afraid to take off. She put her best foot forward to join in socially, but she always turned in early, not feeling fully deserving of having fun. She saw a new therapist to work through the past and support her to make different decisions going forward. She had some days—even some weeks—that she felt better, but the pain kept seeping back in. No matter how many hours she could go without thinking of her hurt, it snuck back on her, like stepping in a puddle of water just after putting on a fresh pair of socks.

She eventually started to date other people. She even had a boyfriend that was a lot of fun, but even after a few years together, she knew deep down that she wasn't in love with him the way she had been with Noah. After another breakup, she promised herself the gift of time to find out what she really wanted. Most of her friends were getting married in what felt like rapid succession to her, and they all seemed to be getting pregnant soon after their honeymoons. She was single, nearing forty, and—although she thought she might like a child someday—she was not in the right headspace, relationship, or financial position to have one.

Afraid that her time might run out, Jillian decided to have her eggs frozen. She spent her savings and took hormone injections, enduring a series of uncomfortable and invasive doctor appointments—all the while hoping that, when she was ready, she would still have the option to have a baby.

On the day of her egg retrieval, she had to find someone to drive her to and from the appointment. Her friend Allison had suffered a miscarriage just two weeks prior, and Jillian had spent the evening comforting Allison the night before her scheduled D&C. Allison wanted to return the favor and take Jillian to her appointment. Although Allison had a healthy three-year-old at home, finding out that what she thought would be her second baby's heart had stopped beating had shocked her system. Allison and Jillian shared the sadness of babies lost and the babies they both hoped for.

After the egg retrieval procedure, Jillian made another decision for the future and chose to start graduate school and study physical therapy. She was ready for change, and she embraced it. It wasn't long after she started her second year of school that her friend wanted to set her up with this guy named Max. She swore that at the very least Jillian would have a fun night. Jillian agreed to go out with him—and although she wasn't sure she was ready to be romantically involved with anyone, let alone a good friend of a friend, she really enjoyed his company. Jillian couldn't remember the last time she'd laughed so hard.

For months after they met, Max pined after Jillian. She loved spending time with him, but she worried: that if she moved things along with him and it didn't work, she could lose him. She also wasn't sure she could be in another relationship again. Max didn't give up, but he also didn't push her. He simply built a strong friendship between them that grew naturally into them being together every day.

One night, Jillian and Max shared a bottle of wine. The two of them were sitting close enough together that Jillian could see the speckles in his blue eyes. Max, giddy from the wine and feeling a bit bolder than usual, said, "If you want a family, you know we can do that." She had told him about freezing her eggs but didn't expect him to bring it back up, since most men would panic when a woman admitted she actually wanted a baby—at least, in her experience.

Jillian laughed at his touching offer but was unsure how she should respond. "Jillian, you want a baby? Let's have a baby," Max said, smiling. He was getting drunk—but so was she, so when he leaned in to kiss her, she didn't back away this time.

It took a few months before Jillian really let herself accept that Max, whom she grew to love, was authentic, sweet, kind, and very much in love with her. Once she did, the two of them were inseparable. They moved in together, and while she finished her master's degree and prepared to get her license to become a physical therapist, Max grew his editing business. Their lives were busy, full, and exciting. Neither one took the positive change for granted. After what felt like years of living in a haze, Jillian felt a brightness to her days. On weekends, they would often get out of the city together, exploring new towns and staying in the desert or the mountains. One weekend while hiking together, Max proposed to Jillian. When she said yes, she was sure she meant it.

Jillian and Max got married a few hours north of Los Angeles. Jillian had her heart set on getting married in a converted bare-boned barn similar to the one she and Noah had chosen when they had planned their wedding. This time, she embraced every decision with the certainty that she would get to enjoy her choices together with Max, her family, and all of their friends. The wedding was a celebration not only of love, but of patience and perseverance. Along with rejoicing, Jillian was relieved that the day had finally come and the heaviness that had followed her for years lightened.

After a few months of newlywed trips, lazy weekends, and enjoying the realization that they were both actually married now. They would call each other using "husband" and "wife" instead of using each other's names. As it all settled in, Jillian remembered the eggs she had frozen, and since she was nearing forty-five, she made an appointment with her fertility doctor. This time Max went with her, both for support and to learn what options they had as partners and as potential parents.

The first step, the fertility doctor said, was to thaw Jillian's frozen eggs to see how many looked viable. Then the fertility specialist would wash the eggs to prepare them for fertilization. Jillian and Max agreed to start the process. They went home and waited for the phone call to update them.

They began with nine frozen eggs—then there were five that looked like they had potential, then two, and then one. As Jillian watched her chances of becoming pregnant with her frozen eggs diminish, she prepared herself for the reality that the last frozen egg wouldn't work either. She wouldn't let herself cry until she heard that it was truly over.

When she got the news, even though she'd prepared for the worst, no amount of preparation was enough. The fertility doctor explained to them that the percentage of eggs being viable to fertilize goes down with age and that increasing a woman's fertility is still a science in progress—a science with no guarantees. She listened to the voice on the other end of the phone and heard every other word. What did the details matter now? She struggled to respond in the right places with the right words. She said "Okay, I see" and "Thank you," but none of these felt authentic to her. When she finally hung up, she slid down to the kitchen floor and cried. Max sat beside her and held her. They didn't say much to each other for the rest of the night. They didn't have to speak—too much had already been said for one day.

A week later, Jillian's fertility doctor called her to discuss other options. He suggested the idea of using a donor egg with Max's sperm: that way, she could still carry the baby. If she wanted to go in this direction, they would have to act soon.

Jillian and Max discussed this possibility but never reached a concrete decision. Max didn't want to adopt—and until he met Jillian, he hadn't seen himself being a father. His own father was absent in his life, and he had his own insecurities about having a child. He was on board to have a child with his wife, but when it didn't happen, he was also okay with letting it go. It was Jillian who struggled with how to proceed. By now she had a growing business, was looking into buying a house, and was happily married. She had a lot—maybe it was enough.

They weren't looking for a dog, but when the opportunity presented itself, Jillian and Max adopted Bully: an adorable three-pound furry terror who seemed to reserve all of his love just for the two of them. Fran the cat, who was getting older, tolerated Bully. When they found a townhouse to buy together in Echo Park, the four of them settled into their new home together. The busyness that came with furnishing, unpacking, and fixing up their first home took up any time that Jillian had to think about a baby. She was smitten with Bully, and he kept her hands full.

When their new home was ready, they began having friends over for game nights, holiday dinners, and impromptu parties. They were proud of what they put into their home and enjoyed entertaining. As time went on, it never seemed like the right time to take steps toward having a baby.

When Fran died, Jillian cried over losing her, and all she had lost since Fran had been in her life. Fran sat with her after every heartbreak, move, and loss—she was the closest thing to a baby Jillian had ever had. She thought about Noah, and how—months after she had made the choice not to keep their baby—he confessed to her that he wanted her to keep it. She had pushed the memory away before, like pushing your head out of the water to take a breath. There was no good to come from knowing what he wanted after the fact. When she cried for Fran, she also cried for the baby she chose not to have and for the baby, she couldn't have when she chose to.

Jillian's decisions about her body were ultimately always hers to make. Both Noah and Max had stepped back and let her make the final call. Now her choices seemed limited, and she was tired of carrying the heaviness of it all on her own. Months turned into years, and she waited for the decision to be made for her: for her window of opportunity to close. As she watched her co-workers, her patients, and her closest friends go through pregnancy, childbirth, and motherhood, she didn't always pine after what they had. She often sat back, observing—and wondering if she wanted to live in their shoes.

The longer she thought about parenthood, the more ambivalence she felt. When she stopped talking about it to her friends, eventually they stopped asking, all ignoring the elephant in the room until he quietly slipped out, unnoticed.

Chapter Four

Daniela

The apartment building in Lawndale where Daniela lived wasn't very exciting. It was a common 1970s-style complex with unkempt hallways that filled with the smells of multiple meals cooking throughout the day. The glass on the front door was scratched, the metal mailboxes were dented, and the walls looked like they hadn't been repainted since the building first opened. But once Daniela unlocked her apartment door, she was home. She lived with her mother, Christina; her mother's boyfriend, Eduardo; her brother, Alejandro; his girlfriend, Veronica; and their four-year-old daughter, Emily. The apartment was a bit on the smaller size, full of all of them living there. It was also full of pure joy.

Christina had moved to California from Mexico to raise her five children. Daniela was her youngest, and they loved each other's company. On Daniela's 18th birthday, Christina and Eduardo threw her a party with the whole family and a few friends. The crepe paper streamers and paper pom poms still hung from the ceiling a few weeks later—Daniela wasn't ready to take them down. She liked how happy they made her, thinking of everyone she loved filling up the apartment and celebrating with her.

Christina woke up early most days to catch the bus to work. She cleaned houses for five different families: her days were long and physically exhausting. The buses never went directly to any of her families' houses, so she had to walk for about twenty minutes before starting to work, then clean for a few hours before walking back to the bus before it got dark. An easy day was when Eduardo didn't work the night shift and could drive her or pick her up. A lucky day was when she had two houses to clean and could bring one of her three daughters with her to help.

Daniela had grown up working alongside her mother at work from time to time. Most of the people her mother worked for were nice, but one family in particular was her favorite. They were always happy to see her when she came along with her mother. There was always music left on for them in Spanish to enjoy while they cleaned, and the family always shared treats with them whenever they came over.

Daniela finished high school just a few months before her birthday and now watched her niece Emily most days when everyone else went to work. She loved watching her niece—it never felt like work. They drew pictures together, played at the park, and had lunch together. One day they raced each other home and walked into the building out of breath. In the hall, Daniela held Emily's hand, swinging it back and forth and giggling when she saw a man standing in front of the door of the apartment next to hers. She couldn't tell how old he was—she knew he was older than her, but young enough to still be cute. She met his eyes and started laughing.

"Hi, sorry! We were just coming back from the park and we were being a little silly," Daniela said. She fumbled through what barely resembled a sentence and realized the man was smiling at her. She felt Emily tug her arm, which shook her out of her trance. She found her keys and smiled back at him before unlocking her door and going inside with Emily.

When they got inside, Daniela felt her heart racing—and it wasn't because she and Emily ran. She wasn't out of breath. She simply felt excited about the guy smiling at her in the hall. She had never seen him before and wanted to know who he was. She tried to think of excuses to go back in the hallway, but he probably would be inside the apartment next door. She tried to think of a reason to knock on that door, but that was too obvious—and she didn't really know her next door neighbors that well, anyway. She wondered if he was curious about her, too. After all, he did smile at her. She wondered how to find another chance to see him but decided the only thing to do was to wait and hope she ran into him again .

A few days later, she was walking back from the pharmacy when she saw him outside the building. She caught his eyes and felt her heart start to race. She could see clearly now that he was actually more than just a few years older than her—he was a man, not some guy like the ones she had hung out with before. He wasn't Latino either; he was Black, with wide shoulders and—even though he looked really strong—there was something sweet in his eyes that Daniela couldn't help noticing.

"Do you need help with any of your bags?" he asked.

"Oh thank you, I'm okay—they're not heavy, it's just some toothpaste and paper towels and stuff. Thank you, though." Daniela stood there with her two white plastic bags hanging from her hands. If she left and went in, she might not see him again for a while. She smiled at him and put her bags down to get her keys out, but also to stall for time.

"I saw you the other day in the hall with your little girl. My family lives next to you guys, I guess."

"That's my niece. My brother's baby."

"Oh, well you are a good auntie then. You two looked like you were having fun." Daniela was glad to be talking to him and wanted to stay outside longer just to keep the conversation going.

"I'm Mikey—I would shake your hand, but they are full," he said. Daniela laughed.

"Nice to meet you. I'm Daniela.

"Nice to meet you, too. Since I can't help you with your bags, at least let me open the door for you." Daniela noticed he had his own keys to the building, so maybe she would get to see him again soon. Mikey unlocked the outside door and held it open for Daniela.

"Thank you."

"You are most welcome. Hopefully, we'll see each other again soon." Mikey said.

Daniela felt like she was burning up. She knew her cheeks must have been red because she felt heat rise from them as she smiled. She quickly replayed every word he had just said, holding onto his words to get her through until the next time she got to see him. She was too afraid to say the wrong thing, so she just kept smiling until she got in, opened her door, and went inside. Daniela tried to take a deep breath as she put her bags down and ran into the bathroom to throw water on her face. She didn't want anyone at home to notice how flushed she was—if they did, they would either tease her or bug her to tell them why. She just wanted to keep this one thing for herself.

Daniela had never had a real boyfriend. She found a few guys attractive but hadn't ever been with anyone for more than a few weeks. She was curious about Mikey and the feeling she felt when she saw him was more than she ever felt for anyone she had liked before. She hoped that maybe he felt curious about her too.

Over the next few weeks, she saw Mikey more often. They would talk outside the building, and he would keep her company while she was watching Emily. Once, when they were crossing the street, he put his hand on her shoulder to help them get across safely. Daniela knew that meant he cared about her.

Mikey kept Daniela company for an hour here and there during the week when he could. She noticed that, as the weeks went by, he would show up more often. Once while watching Emily at the park his hand brushed beside hers and his pinky reached for hers. They sat on the bench with their pinkies linked, and Daniela felt that heat return to her cheeks. She had been telling herself that maybe he liked her more than a friend, but until this moment she couldn't be sure.

Daniela and Mikey figured out ways to spend time together. Despite having little privacy, they were able to find places to fool around: sometimes they kissed while leaning against the side of the building. Even though Daniela learned Mikey was thirty, it didn't change how she felt about him. He wanted to be with her, and she wanted to be with him. Her family had a feeling that she was seeing him, even though she never told them. Their concern was not just his age, but that he was Black. There was a lot of fighting between Black and Brown communities in LA, and Daniela's family thought it would be safer to keep their distance. They weren't all legal, some of the family members were undocumented, and they didn't need any extra reasons to cause trouble. Daniela knew all of this, but her feelings for Mikey were too strong to ignore.

Very few people used the building's stairwell—and if people did come in, they had to push a loud, crashing door before getting to the stairs. This allowed Mikey and Daniela some privacy, and the stairs became their new spot. The first time they had sex, they were able to be alone in Daniela's apartment. It was Daniela's first time and Mikey was gentle, slow, and kind. Afterward, Daniela smiled, and Mikey joked around with her about her not being a virgin anymore.

It was rare for either of them to have an apartment to themselves so after that, they had to be more creative with where to go. They had sex once up against the wall of the stairwell. It wasn't as romantic as some of the other times, but it was exciting to be doing something so private in a public place while listening out for the doors to open.

Daniela had learned about safe sex in her high school health class. Over and over, they talked about condoms but neither she nor Mikey ever had any—plus, it was so hard to stop what they were doing at the moment and put one on. Daniella trusted that Mikey was safe. She figured she was aware of her cycle, so she thought they would be okay.

When her period didn't come for a month, she didn't worry about it, but when two *more* weeks went by, she walked down to the pharmacy to get a pregnancy test. She didn't tell anyone she was getting one, not even Mikey. When she took the test and it was positive, she became terrified. She cried, unsure what to do. She didn't want to tell her family, especially her mother, because she was worried that Christina would be so angry with her. She decided to tell her sister first because it would be easier—and when she did, her sister encouraged her to tell her mother.

Daniela could not stop crying when she tried to talk to her mother. She hid her face in her hands as she struggled to speak: every time she tried to say anything, she just cried harder. Finally, she looked up at her mother and could see that her mother was afraid. The idea that she was hurting or scaring her mother was not something she could handle.

"Daniela, you have to tell me what is going on," Christina said. Daniela tried to take a deep breath to begin, but before she could say anything her mother started speaking again. "Are you pregnant?" Christina asked. Daniela looked up at her mother and started sobbing. Christina hugged her, and that kindness gave Daniela enough strength to speak.

"Yes, I am," she said. Christina hugged her even tighter. "I am so sorry, mama."

"Calm down—you are pregnant, it is not the end of the world, and we will figure it out. Your life is going to change, and this is a big responsibility. You are going to be a mom soon, and that means you are going to have to learn to provide for that little baby growing inside you." When she heard that, Daniela looked up and nodded, and suddenly snapped into reality. Her mother's words were true: she would have to start making enough money to buy everything her baby would need. Christina said Daniela could start working with her and cleaning. She also said she would save a little bit of her earnings to help Daniela. Daniela hugged her mother and sank into her chest, grateful to have her love and her help.

"Mikey, I want you to know something," Daniela said

"Okay," Mikey said suspiciously. Daniela sat Mikey down on the couch and sat down next to him.

"I'm pregnant. You are going to be a daddy." Daniella said

"How far along are you?" Mikey asked She didn't know but had made a doctor's appointment and wanted to know if he wanted to come. He did, which made her happy.

At the appointment, they learned that Daniela was four months along. The doctor did an ultrasound, revealing to an amazed Daniela a tiny baby that looked fully formed. She could see the baby's head, spine, the cutest little butt, thighs, shins, feet, and hands. The heartbeat was so strong, so fast—and with that sound, she felt love surrounding her. A sense of lucidity in her identity and who she would become settled within her: in that moment, she became a mother. She hadn't had any morning sickness or any other symptoms, but as soon as she knew she was pregnant, her body sang it out. She got it all: vomiting, swelling, and stretch marks, symptoms that lasted until she was six months along. Her belly grew fast after that, and at her next ultrasound, she and Mikey could see they would be having a boy.

Daniela was so proud to be pregnant. She enjoyed showing off her baby bump and loved feeling her little boy kicking around. As her last month approached, she began to feel Braxton Hicks contractions. They felt like a bicycle tire being pumped with air and then a wave breaking over her belly as it released. Her due date was April 30th, but it was only the end of March.

Daniela returned to the doctor on April 12th and was told that it was almost time to deliver. They sent her home and instructed her to come back a few days later. Knowing she was going to be giving birth soon, she asked her mom if they could go to Target to buy a few things that she still needed for the baby; on the way, Christina offered to treat her to a caramel Frappuccino: the Venti size, since it was a special occasion. Daniela drank it slowly so she could savor it.

The day that Daniela was supposed to go to the hospital, her family all went out to dinner together to celebrate Mikey's birthday. Daniela looked around the table at her family celebrating Mikey. She placed her hand over her belly and thought about how, soon enough, there would be one more joining their family.

The next day, Christina helped Daniela pack her baby bag and gave her a special tea to help with the birth. Christina had to work, but she drove her baby Daniela to the hospital so she could have her own baby.

"I have only one house to clean today, so tell that baby boy to wait for me to come back," Christina said. Daniela laughed and entered the hospital to be admitted. Upon examination, she learned she was already six centimeters dilated. Everyone in the room kept asking her if she was okay or if she needed anything—and she kept telling them that she was fine, she felt great, she was just excited.

After a few hours, the doctor came and broke her water. He said he would check back with her after completing another patient's cesarean section. Right after he left, Daniela's contractions got intense; about an hour into them, Daniela called Christina to come back because it wouldn't be much longer before the baby would be out.

"Wait for me, little baby," Christina said.

"Grandma Stina wants you to wait for her, little one, and she is the boss, so you have to listen," Daniela instructed her belly.

The nurses in the room thought that was funny—and when they laughed, Daniela started to laugh too. She was still giggling when they checked her again and discovered she was already eight centimeters dilated. It seemed like everyone in her family started to call her to ask her if the baby was out, and every time she was asked, she started to laugh again.

When the nurses checked her again, Daniela was crowning, but the doctor still hadn't returned. The nurses kept calling him, and finally, he ran back into the room. As he washed his hands and put gloves on, he explained that he was in the cafeteria getting a coffee. While Daniela thought that was funny, the nurses had a sense of urgency.

Daniela got even more excited knowing she would meet her baby boy soon. As the doctor tied his paper gown, Daniela laughed again, maybe from excitement and nerves. Whatever it was, she didn't seem to be able to stop. The doctor paused for a second to look at his giddy patient.

"Doctor, please hurry. This girl is going to laugh the baby out," said one of the nurses.

This made everyone in the room laugh, and when the doctor came over to deliver the baby, his job was practically already done. Daniela pushed three times and her baby was out and placed on her chest. He was the most beautiful thing Daniela had ever seen. He was bigger than she thought he would be since he was early. She marveled at his perfect details: his chocolate-brown curly hair, his eyes, his mouth...there was so much for her to discover. She couldn't take her eyes off of him and didn't want to let him go to be weighed or measured, but she was curious. He weighed seven pounds, five ounces, and was twenty-one and a half inches long. She held him in her arms, only releasing him again to let her mother hold him when she arrived.

Mikey and Daniela named their baby Evan.

Christina had taught Daniela the importance of the first forty days of the baby's life. She explained that what a mother eats, where you go, and what the baby wears all factor into the health of the baby.

When they got to take Evan home from the hospital, Daniela carefully dressed him in new little cotton leggings to go over a onesie before putting him into his new car seat. Daniela and Evan would be living at home with Christina, so Daniela knew that, once she got home, they probably would be staying in for most of those forty days. She and Mikey decided to stop at In-N-Out for a cheeseburger, fries, and a shake, knowing that her future held a bland diet. They went through the drive-in, got their food, and then took it to a park to eat it outside while Evan sat beside them in his stroller. The food tasted especially delicious to Daniela after having a baby and then eating hospital food for a day.

When the new family arrived back home, there was a surprise waiting for Daniela. Her grandparents had come up from Mexico to welcome the baby. Christina had *atole* ready for them to all drink together—one of Daniela's favorite drinks. *Atole* is a Mexican drink made from the liquid that grits are cooked in, and it is known to help with milk production. It would be a few more days before Daniela would confess to her mother that she had been stuffed full of In-N-Out, which her mother scolded her for.

"Everything you ate was bad for the baby. You are not supposed to eat dairy or potatoes—and what was the baby wearing when you were out?" Christina asked

"I wrapped him in a blanket."

"He is too little for you to have him out and about with only his thin cotton clothes."

"I'm sorry, Mama," said Daniela.

Now that she was home, Daniela was able to focus entirely on Evan. She knew her mother was right and decided to take the forty days seriously from that point forward. She ate a lot of boring food like oatmeal and soup—but she also had no issues with the baby nursing, so it was working. Christina offered to watch Evan a few times or to pick him up whenever he cried, but Daniela wanted to do everything for him.

Christina grew impressed with what a responsible mother Daniela was becoming. She had thought that she was going to have to help raise Evan and teach Daniela how to care for him, but she was pleasantly surprised at how nurturing Daniela was. She could see how beautiful the bond between them was. She was proud of what a loving mother Daniela was, and it gave her immense joy to watch them together.

For the first three months of Evan's life, Mikey and Daniela lived at home with Christina. Daniela went to work with Christina so that she could make enough money to care for Evan but also so that she and Mikey could move into an apartment together someday. Daniela would bring Evan with her whenever she cleaned because she didn't want to be away from him. Since she and her mom were working together, she was able to take breaks if she needed to nurse or change the baby. She also liked bringing him with her so she could show anyone and everyone this beautiful little boy she made. She loved sharing him with others and would glow when he was admired.

Christina enjoyed having Evan and Daniela around her. She had other grandchildren and she loved them all, but there was something magical about seeing her baby holding her own baby. It made her realize that, although she would never be done being a mother to her children, a big portion of her responsibility for them was lifted from her. She could see that all of her five children were going to be fine on their own. She would always be there for them when they asked for her, but they didn't need her in the same way they used to. This realization was something Christina thought might be melancholy, but it was actually the opposite. She saw that her years of commitment to parenting her children had made them responsible young adults.

Daniela's world became Evan and being a mom changed her in the best possible way. Everyone in her family could see the maturity in her. When she was home, she would let her brothers and sisters hold the baby—but when it came to meeting any of his needs, she wanted to be the one to tend to him. She didn't want to miss any experience with him because he was hers, and she loved that fact. She would sometimes hold him while he was only in a diaper and then put him under her oversized tee shirt with his little head sticking out. She would just lie still, holding him skin-to-skin while wrapping his curls around her fingers. For as much as she held him, she thought he would cry when she had to put him down, but he was never fussy. He just seemed content to be near her.

Mikey had wanted the three of them to move in together as a family, but Christina had told Daniela to wait the first few months and live at home. Christina wanted to be sure that Mikey would stay in the relationship. Daniela's family liked Mikey, but they weren't always so welcoming to him. When she got pregnant, they were upset that she wouldn't have a Hispanic baby. Over time, though, they all got to know Mikey. He was polite and kind, and the family could see that he cared deeply for Daniela.

After three months of living at home, Mikey asked Daniela to move in with him again, and this time, Christina agreed to let them go. Mikey found them an apartment about forty-five minutes away from Christina—which felt far, but they agreed to stop home whenever they came back for Evan's doctor appointments.

Being away on her own for the first time wasn't as hard as Daniela thought it might be. She had her own family now, her own home, and two people she loved very much who depended on her. Mikey was able to take time off from work because they offered him paternity leave, so he took it and they settled into a new neighborhood together. Daniela knew no one, but she would walk Evan down the convenience store each day. There, she got to know the cashiers, who fawned over Evan every time he came in, telling Daniela that he was the most handsome baby they had ever seen. She spent her days walking to one or two of three stores near their apartment. That was all she was able to do each day, and she didn't mind one bit.

At around four months old, Evan was so smiley that it was hard for Daniela to resist his smile and leave his side. Mikey and Daniela had this ongoing joke between them about Evan's hair. He had soft, full curls, and Mikey liked to wet a brush to run through them, straightening them down as he went. As soon as Daniela saw him, she would re-curl his hair by wrapping her fingers back around strands. One day they did his hair from straight to curls three times before they both gave up, laughing.

Evan still woke up during the night to nurse around one in the morning, and then he would sleep again until about five. Mikey and Daniela started putting Evan in his own crib so that they could sit together on the couch to watch a movie. Before putting him to bed, they would let him sit with them for a little bit together. One night, Evan didn't seem to want to be held or put down and only seemed happy when both Mikey and Daniela sat on either side of him. He commanded their affection by reaching for both of them that night. When Daniela finally got up to take a bath before putting Evan to bed, he didn't seem to want to let her go. He kept smiling at her, and when she walked away, he would whine a little. She put him in his bouncy seat and took a bath. When she came out, Evan was asleep, and Daniela was impressed that he was able to self-soothe himself to sleep. She kissed his sweet-smelling cheek as she lifted him into his crib. She placed him down and rubbed his back to make sure he didn't wake up after she let go of him. Then she left the room to sit with Mikey to watch TV; shortly after that, they both fell asleep with the TV still on.

Daniela kept feeling Evan's hand brush across her face, but when she opened her eyes, she realized she was only dreaming. At one point, she opened her eyes to see the sunlight come through the space between the shade and the window frame, but it didn't make sense that it would be so bright at that angle. Her confusion awakened her as she adjusted to the idea that maybe that light meant it was morning. She felt the weight of her full breasts ache from not being emptied for the usual middle-of-the-night feeding. She jumped off the couch and ran into Evan's room, screaming to Mikey, who didn't understand why she was so upset. She picked him up to wake him, but he wouldn't open his eyes or move.

"Get the phone, Mikey, and call 911," Daniela screamed. Mikey ran back with the phone but seemed to have forgotten how to speak because he was staring at his son in shock.

"Give it to me, Mikey." Daniela dialed and spoke with someone who seemed to ask her too many questions at the most inconvenient time.

"Did he choke on something? Does he have a fever? Has he had any seizures in the past? Is he breathing at all?"

"No, no, not any, and he is not breathing, please, what do I do?" Daniela screamed.

The operator instructed her to perform CPR on her baby and told her that the paramedics would be there soon. She yelled at Mikey to open the door for them and pumped and pumped her baby's chest until they came.

When the paramedics arrived, they found Daniela on the floor with Evan and asked her to leave the room so they could try to help him—but she would not, could not leave him. She sat crying on the bed as they worked on him, barely remembering to breathe herself. It was only a few minutes, but to Daniela and Mikey, it felt like hours before they swept up Evan and instructed them all to ride in the ambulance to the hospital.

All that Daniela remembered hearing them say when they wheeled Evan into the hospital was "Baby is six months old, unconscious, with a faint pulse." Then he was whisked away, and Daniela and Mikey were separated. At the hospital, there were police officers who put Daniela and Mikey in different rooms so that they could be questioned. She realized very quickly how serious Evan's situation was. She kept begging to see Evan, or for someone to tell her what was happening, but instead, she had to answer question after question from an officer with no facial expressions. Given the situation, he seemed so quiet and still with his questioning. This man's calm unsettled Daniela, whose every part was screaming. How could he just sit there asking her for answers? Based on his questions it was if he suspected she or Mikey could have hurt their own son. He had no understanding of how she only longed to hold her baby, to see him, and to know if he was okay.

It felt like forever before anyone came in to give her news. Finally, two nurses came into the room where Daniela had been waiting for so long, and their facial expressions spoke louder than the words coming out of their mouths:

"I'm so sorry, your baby is gone."

Daniela dropped to the floor, pulled her knees into her chest, and sobbed into the flannel shirt that she had pulled on earlier in her haste to get to the hospital. She had been alone in that room, but now she felt alone in the world. Her baby was gone, and she wished she could be gone with him. She wondered where Mikey was, and if he knew. She had questions of her own, but she saw no end to her sitting on the floor. Her head and heart were racing. She tried to adjust her position on the floor but as soon as she moved, she convulsed and vomited. The nurses helped lift her onto a chair and gave her napkins to wipe her mouth and a cup of water to sip.

"Can I please see my baby?" Daniela managed to ask.

The nurses asked her to give them a moment and then one of them left the room. When the nurse returned, she asked Daniela who she would like to no-tify about Evan, and until that moment she had forgotten about anyone else in her life other than her son. She asked them to please call her mother. It wasn't until Christina arrived at the hospital that the staff allowed Daniela to see Evan. Christina ran into the room and saw Daniela, and they both cried in each other's arms. It seemed that Daniela was finally able to inhale once she was in her mother's arms—the familiar smell of her clothes and hair offered her a fraction of comfort and connection.

The hospital staff asked Christina to come outside to talk before visiting Evan. When they told Mikey that Evan had died, they shared, Mikey had asked to see the baby. He picked Evan up, wrapped him, and started to leave. Mikey explained to everyone as he tried to take home his baby that Evan was fine, and it was all a big misunderstanding. The staff explained to Christina as she wept that Mikey was in shock, as well as Daniela, and that seeing the baby would most certainly upset her more. Christina needed to be aware that she might have to hold her daughter up, they said.

Before she and Christina could go into the room, Daniela was told that she was not allowed to touch Evan: she could go in and look at him, but she could not pick him up. Daniela agreed, and they were led to a small, dim room where Evan had been wheeled. He was swaddled neatly in a clean white sheet. His eyes were closed, and he looked asleep—but right away Daniela saw that his lips were a purplish color. She immediately regretted agreeing to not touch him. It seemed like an impossible request to ask of her. This was her baby, and she longed for him. As soon as she stepped forward to reach for him, she was pulled back. That was the last time she saw Evan before his funeral.

Daniela doesn't remember much about leaving the hospital that day, except that she left without Evan. She, Mikey, and Christina were reunited, but none of them could find the energy or the words to speak to each other. It was recommended that Daniela not return to the apartment right away, especially not to go into Evan's room. Christina collected a few of her daughter's things and took Daniela back to her house. Her grandparents were visiting again; they hadn't been to California since Evan was born.

"I'm so sorry, mama, that your grandmother and I were here to welcome your little one into the world and for him to leave it," Daniela's grandfather said.

An autopsy was performed, and within a few days, Daniela received a phone call with the results. The cause of death was Sudden Infant Death Syndrome, or SIDS: the unexplained death of a seemingly healthy baby in their sleep, sometimes caused by toys or blankets in the crib. Evan had a blanket—but it was nowhere near his face, so she knew it hadn't been the cause. She learned later that some babies just forget to breathe, or that they don't wake up enough to take in a breath. She learned that teaching babies to take a pacifier helps because it forces them to breathe through their noses. She went over a million things that she could have done differently the months before, the week before, and the night before Evan's death that would have kept him alive. If only she didn't leave him to take a bath when he smiled at her the night before, he would still be here. If only he didn't fall asleep on his own, she would have held him longer. If only, if only.

It was never clear why the sun shone through the apartment that day at what seemed an impossible angle, or why Daniela had been visited in dreams that night of Evan's hand brushing across her face. Both of those unresolved moments felt like him saying goodbye.

A few weeks after Evan's death, Daniela learned that she was pregnant again. She had suspected the news a few weeks before and remembered telling Evan that maybe he would become a big brother soon. As her second son grew stronger inside her, her relationship with Mikey cracked apart. Evan's death was not either of their faults—but they couldn't help blaming each other for the pain and loss.

Daniela gave birth to a healthy baby boy. Mikey met his son Mateo a few times, but every time he visited, his mind flashed back to losing Evan. Daniela believed they might have lasted if it wasn't for Evan's death—the pain was just too sharp and the memories too strong to remain together. Mikey's visits to his new baby grew further and further apart. He tried to stay living in the apartment, but he couldn't walk by the closed door to Evan's old room without getting pulled back to that devastating morning. He moved away, and although Daniela never missed a moment with her new baby, she understood why Mikey needed to leave.

Eventually, she met someone new, got married, and went on to have three more children. John, her husband has raised Mateo along with his own. Whenever Daniela still wonders about Evan and questions her choices that night, she looks to her children, knowing that they are all here because Evan made her the mother she is. She sees facial expressions in her children that remind her of Evan—and one of her daughters even has his same eyes. She feels at peace knowing that he lives on in them.

Chapter Five

Norah

Norah and her husband Dylan had been married for five years before deciding to start a family. They were in their late twenties with a dog named Atlas, a nice apartment, and friends they saw regularly. Both were starting to build their careers: Dylan as an art director and Norah as a filmmaker. They both loved their work and their colleagues.

For Norah's thirtieth birthday, she and Dylan threw a fete on the patio of their new house in the West Hollywood hills. As Norah blew out the candles on her cake, she wished that her new decade would bring success, surprises, and a baby.

When Norah and Dylan began to try to have a child, they got pregnant right away. Norah had that pregnancy glow that women talked about. She felt amazing—she had no morning sickness and her skin and hair were refreshed and full. Instead of feeling exhausted, she actually felt more energized. She absolutely loved being pregnant.

Norah had always taken care of herself. She preferred natural, healthy products and foods and was careful to stay away from preservatives, pesticides, and inorganic produce. She wanted to be even more mindful of these choices while she was pregnant, as she didn't want to put anything into her body that could be toxic to her baby. Norah also wanted to have the baby without any medication, if possible. She read books on hospital births versus home births and grew determined to have their baby at home. Dylan supported her decision, and after a careful interviewing process, they chose a midwife.

With their birth plan now set, Norah and Dylan created a small nursery by partitioning a small section of their bedroom. Dylan was quite good at woodworking, and Norah had a great eye for design. For colors, they chose different shades of sage green, light brown, and burnt orange. They had decided to wait until the baby was born to find out the gender, and neither liked the idea of using a palette of colors that were meant for one gender or the other. When the little room was completed, it felt warm and welcoming. The room let in soft light without being jarringly bright. Proudly, the two of them considered their work.

Dylan leaned down to speak directly to Norah's belly. "We make a good team, the three of us," he said as he kissed them both. Norah smiled back excitedly.

"I can't believe we are actually going to do this. I'm getting a little scared.," Norah admitted.

Wrapping her in his arms, Dylan looked into her eyes. "We are committed now," he joked. "You are the strongest woman out there, babe. We got this."

Norah and Dylan spent the next few weeks preparing for the baby's arrival, and while they waited, they went to the movies, ate at their favorite restaurants, and made plans with their friends. Norah's friend Carly threw her a baby shower complete with a blessing circle: her friends passed around a bowl and placed notes, necklaces, and charms inside it for Norah to have near her during the birth. Norah's belly was front and center as she neared the end of the pregnancy. As her girlfriends surrounded her, they each shared words of encouragement and toasted her. Carly gave each guest a candle to take home and explained that it was to light when Norah went into labor. Carly had set up a phone tree and would let everyone know when the right time was. Norah's mother, who was French Israeli and always direct, joined the shower from San Diego. She looked down at the candle in her hand.

"Is this candle supposed to make the baby come out easily?" she asked, and by her tone, no one was quite sure if she was joking or not.

"That would be lovely, but it is just the idea that we are all united in sending her positive energy while she gives birth," Carly offered. She was authentic in her efforts to help her friend transition into motherhood as smoothly as possible. Although Carly didn't have any of her own children yet, she wanted one at some point soon, and she understood that giving birth could be both scary and magical all at once. She wanted to let Norah know that, even though all of the women who loved her couldn't be in the birthing room with her physically, they would be there in spirit.

"What if I miss the call when she goes into labor, and I don't get to light my candle?" Norah's mother asked. "Will you keep calling those of us who miss the first call?"

"Yes, if you would like, I can make sure that you get the message," Carly said. Norah's mother gave a half nod and seemed content enough with that.

Ten days before her due date, Norah was walking Atlas when she felt a trail of liquid run down her leg. Looking around self-consciously, she checked to see that no one was watching her. She thought she peed a little without even realizing it. Her belly was so big, and there was so much going on below her chest that she could barely see anymore, so it wasn't out of the realm of possibility. She started to walk home quickly so that she could get back to privacy and a toilet.

When she went to the bathroom, she took her pants off and realized she still felt fluid trailing her legs. It was only then that she realized her water was breaking. She stood there, immobilized by this realization. She knew she had to do something and after being still for what felt like minutes to her, she looked for her phone. With shaky hands, she started to look for the midwife's name, but she couldn't remember it—her mind was racing. She didn't have everything set up in the living room yet. Did she want to be in the living room or the bedroom? She suddenly thought about getting into bed and taking a minute to think before realizing she hadn't told Dylan yet.

"Dylan, my water broke—how far away are you?" Norah asked.

"Already?" Wow—okay, um, I can drive home in about half an hour. Will you be okay?" Dylan asked.

"I don't know, I've never done this before," she replied matter-of-factly.

After hanging up, the name Anna popped into Norah's head—Anna was her midwife's name. She found the contact in her phone and called to let her know her water had broken. Within twenty minutes, Anna was at her door. Norah had moved herself into the living room and Dylan came home shortly after. He helped set up cushions and towels to have on hand while Norah's labor intensified.

Norah's contractions grew closer together soon after Anna arrived. Norah felt a tremendous relief to have Anna there, keeping track of her contractions and helping her with her breathing. Things moved quickly —in just over two hours, Norah began to push. She felt the urge to push, but after practicing breathing for so long, her first few attempts at pushing were just big exhales. Her mouth was shaped in a circle, and she pushed the air out of her lungs as if she was trying to create enough of a breeze to move a feather across the room.

Anna instructed her firmly. "Norah, you need to bear down and direct your pushes. You are just breathing now—you need to think about where the baby is and help move it."

Norah gave a big push, and both Anna and Dylan cheered her on. "That's it, Norah, can you give me a few more just like that?" Anna asked.

Norah couldn't find the energy or the words to answer since all of her was focused on pushing, but she heard Anna and felt in a zone with her. Like a steep hike, she wasn't going to stop until she reached the top. Keeping her head straight ahead, Norah listened to every instruction about when to breathe and when to push. She could hear Anna say that she could see the baby's head, and she could feel Dylan's hand on her forehead as she continued breathing and pushing.

"You are right there, Norah, one last push," Anna coached her along. With one last push, Norah told herself *you're actually doing this*. This experience was way more intense than she ever imagined—but she was making it through.

"Norah, go ahead—reach down and grab your baby," Anna guided. Norah brought her shaky hands down between her legs and felt her way to her beautiful baby.

Anna wrapped the baby and helped Dylan cut the cord. They stared at the baby, marveling at its fully formed face and listening to its tiny sounds. Dylan turned to Anna and asked, "Is it a boy or a girl?" They were so enthralled with their tiny new human that they had forgotten all about it having a gender.

"I haven't looked yet. You tell us," Anna replied. Dylan and Norah looked at each other and then Dylan slowly unfolded the blanket that held their new baby.

He got a good look and made sure that Norah could see as well. They both smiled and wrapped the blanket back up.

"It's a boy!" Norah exclaimed. As they marveled at all of the details of their new baby boy, Norah tried to take it all in. Fingers with fingernails, miniature joints, two nostrils, two eyes, the swirl of fine hair on the top of his head. It amazed her that she grew this little person all of these months and it actually worked. She was able to nurse him easily from her first attempt, which she had been told could be challenging. As she cradled him, feeling his weight in her arms, she tried to acquaint herself with the baby in her arms and connect him to the baby she had carried.

The birth had happened so fast that the whole phone tree idea never happened. When Norah called her mother to let her know she was a grandma now, Norah had to hold the phone away from her ear because her mother was yelling so happily. She then asked "No phone call, no candle? What happened?"

Norah had to explain that no one was called and promised her mother that she was the first one to be notified. "I am flattered—so when do I get to meet my grandson?"

"Mom, let me get through the first night with him and we can check back in after that," said Norah. She then remembered to call Carly to let her know that the baby was born and that the birth went well. Carly congratulated her and reassured her that she would let everyone know, then asked to come by and see the baby once Norah was ready for guests.

When Norah hung up the phone, she looked at her baby sleeping snugly in the middle of the blanket laid out on the floor. She wasn't quite sure when she would be ready for the outside world—she only knew that, at this moment, she didn't want to go anywhere or do anything but get to know her baby.

After three days with their son, Norah and Dylan decided to name him Asher. Asher made them a family. He was an easy baby, and the adjustment to motherhood had gone smoothly for Norah. Having always been a fairly even person, she didn't feel any shifts in her mood, baby blues, or any existential panic about how much this baby would change her life. Other than a bit of lower back pain from pushing so hard, she healed physically from giving birth quickly.

Dylan was thrilled to be a father, and the baby anchored him into being present. His high energy and ever-changing mind had served him well creatively, but sometimes Norah wished his attention would hold long enough for him to finish a story. He would go off on tangents and lose his train of thought—she would joke with him and tell him to "stay on target." But holding Asher focused Dylan. Norah witnessed her husband lock eyes with his son and couldn't get enough of how connected they were. She cherished every detail and every day. She was tired—and sometimes, she didn't get to the piles of laundry building up—but she was happy.

Every "first" of Asher's first year was documented on film, edited, and set to music by Norah and Dylan. They loved making films before Asher came—naturally, he became their perfect little subject at home. His walking, his talking, his smiles, and his laughter were all celebrated by the three of them. They nurtured his interests and hobbies, and he grew into an inquisitive toddler with an incredible ability to focus.

Asher loved meeting new people and would take his time studying new faces. Norah read a lot of parenting books and attended a few classes whose philosophy was to raise children to be independent from a very young age. She learned to let her son explore his surroundings, to let him discover playing without adult interruption, and to follow his lead on what he needed. Norah found this style of parenting to work well for them, as it provided her a chance to witness seeing her son take in all the newness around him.

When Asher was three years old, he started going to a small preschool for a few hours each morning. On his first day, Norah brought some yarn to crochet because Laura, the woman who ran the school—a confident, yet gentle earthy type—had suggested she stay for part of the morning. Norah sat on the deck watching Asher play with the other little children while she tried to loop the yarn around her crochet needle to stitch another line of a scarf. She hadn't been sitting long before Laura walked up and said "Mama, I think you can go. He is playing quite nicely here and seems to be content to stay."

Norah sat in her car alone for what felt like the first time since she had Asher. She stared straight ahead while tears filled her eyes until she had to blink to let them fall. As soon as she did, the next batch brimmed in her eyes again. Norah understood that it was time for both Asher and for herself to have some space from one another, but she didn't know how hard it would be to leave him. She took out a notebook and wrote a list of things she could do with this new time she had. She would eventually go back to work, but on that first day, after jotting down a few ideas, she sat in her car drawing little pictures of birds while she waited for the moment to pick Asher up.

Dylan and Norah were the first of their friends to start a family. Other than Dylan's boss—who had four children, all via a surrogate—they didn't know many others with kids yet. When Carly shared with Norah that she and her husband were going to start trying, Norah was so excited for them to become parents. After a few months of fruitless attempts to conceive, Carly shared with Norah that they were having trouble. They tried a few rounds of IVF next, but they remained unsuccessful.

Knowing that Dylan's boss had used a surrogate, Carly asked Norah what she knew about the process. Norah couldn't imagine her life without Asher in it and wanted her friend to have the chance to be a mother. At that moment, a seed was planted in Norah's head: to help Carly, if she could, by offering her womb as if she were offering Carly a place to stay that night.

Many of the three-year-olds that Asher went to school with had baby brothers or sisters. It seemed that the children without siblings were picked up increasingly by pregnant moms. Dylan and Norah hadn't even talked about having another baby. After seeing so many other women around her each day, Norah started to wonder if they should have another baby.

"Do you want a second child, Dylan?" Norah asked.

"I don't know, do you?" Dylan replied.

He was hesitant because their lives had been going so well. What if adding a new baby messed with it all? Plus, he knew more than one family member who got divorced when they had their second child. He thought it might just add too much stress. He didn't want to say all this to Norah in case she had her heart set on having another baby—but if it were up to him, they would quit while they were ahead.

"I'm not really sure," Norah said. She really hadn't decided one way or another, so they let the months pass them by—and when they got antsy, they got a new dog. Having a new baby was something Norah couldn't quite imagine, but she had loved being pregnant. It was just raising another human that she wasn't so sure about.

Carly had ultimately turned down Norah's kind gesture in an effort to protect their friendship. She did eventually find a surrogate with no emotional strings attached, and when Carly welcomed her baby girl into the world, Norah was there to watch the baby being handed to Carly. As she witnessed her friend's long journey into motherhood finally come to a sweet ending, Norah became certain that she wanted to help another woman get there too.

With Dylan on board, Norah began researching information about becoming a surrogate. She began working with an agency that would pair her with potential parents. The first step was filling out the legal paperwork. Next, she had an exam to make sure she was physically and emotionally fit. Some of the requirements were that she'd already had a healthy pregnancy, she wasn't on any antidepressants or anxiety medication, she was between twenty-one and forty years old, she had a child living at home, and she had a healthy BMI. Once she was deemed fit enough, she and Dylan filled out the applications that stated that they were both on board with the decision. The agency approved all the paperwork, and they began looking for matches for Norah. After several months, Norah was paired with a couple who could not have a child of their own. The couple was in their late forties and wanted to use the husband's sperm, a donor egg, and a surrogate to have the baby.

With all the plans in place, Norah and Dylan now needed to share the news with their families. Asher was close to seven, and before they told him, they wanted to make sure he didn't accidentally say anything to her parents, so Norah and Dylan started there. Their responses were mixed. Her father sat quietly without saying much. When he finally did speak, he had several questions. Norah broke down the process for him as best as she could.

"So basically, you are the oven for someone else's bread—and when it's baked, you are going to give it to them?" he asked.

"I suppose so, yes, but we are talking about a baby for them, not a loaf of bread," Norah said.

"Yes, I got that, but just so I understand—you are the oven and the baker." He smiled. Norah laughed and knew to leave it at that with her father.

"If you are going to do all that and have a baby, why shouldn't it be my next grandchild?" Norah's mother asked. Norah would have to work on helping her mother understand over time. When Dylan called to tell his parents, they also had a lot of questions.

"You will be paid for this generosity, yes?" his father asked. "Because if you need money, you can talk to us."

Dylan reassured his father that they weren't doing this for the money and explained that Norah just wanted to help someone else have a baby. It was going to take time for everyone to wrap their heads around the idea of surrogacy—even so, Norah and Dylan were relieved to have shared the news with them.

As their plans progressed, Dylan decided it was time to let Asher know as well. They explained that not everyone was able to have a baby on their own, so Mommy is going to help two people who want to have a baby but have been having trouble. They told him that Mommy would grow the baby for them and then when it is big enough to come out, she will give it to the new parents.

"I am going to have a baby brother or sister?" Asher asked.

"Mommy will have a baby, but she is going to be what is called a surrogate and the baby will grow inside her, but it won't be our baby," Dylan replied.

"So, I am going to have a surrogate baby brother or sister?" Asher asked this time. There would be plenty of time for him to process this once Norah was pregnant, so they nodded in agreement with him.

Getting pregnant this time was far more complicated than when she got pregnant the first time. She had to take hormones to prepare her body to receive the embryo that a doctor would implant during the embryo transfer procedure. After careful planning to coordinate her cycle and align it to match the readiness of the embryo, a date was set. After the procedure, she had to rest to give the embryo the best chance at success. During the next two weeks, she and Dylan had to wait, along with the intended parents, to see if she got pregnant. As when she and Dylan got pregnant with Asher, Norah got pregnant on her first try as a surrogate. She had been told that it wasn't always successful the first time, so Norah took that as a sign that she had made the right decision.

Norah looked forward to being pregnant again, but this pregnancy started out much harder than her first time. She experienced morning sickness for the first time. She threw up and was disappointed to learn, when she did again the next day, that it was becoming a daily occurrence. She didn't carry the same way she did with Asher, with her belly growing straight out in front of her—this baby seemed to make itself obvious right away. Norah felt swollen and uncomfortable.

The parents chose to find out the baby's gender, and when Norah went in for her next ultrasound, she watched as the warm, slick wand slid across her belly. This couple standing in the room with her, eagerly awaiting any details about the baby growing inside of Norah, suddenly felt so foreign to her. When the technician showed them the screen and pointed out what she defined as the "family's jewels" and said, "Looks like you have a little boy in there," the couple behind her sighed with joy so loudly that Norah was too distracted to have any reaction of her own. She never felt afraid that she would get attached to the baby, but she didn't expect to suddenly feel claustrophobic by its presence inside her. It was always clear in her mind that this baby was *their* baby—but watching them look past her to see the monitor reminded her of her father's comment about Norah being the oven. At that moment, she truly felt like one.

Later that night, as Norah was lying in her bed having ice cream, the baby started kicking and Norah started to cry. When Dylan saw his wife crying over her bowl of cookies and cream, he slid behind her on the bed and wrapped his arms around her shoulders. She leaned her head back to rest on his chest.

"These people want to know all the details about this little boy, but then when I am home and he is moving like crazy, they won't ever get to feel what that is like."

"They get to have a baby when he is fully cooked, and that is what they really want," Dylan said.

"I've been fine with this whole thing, and I am not saying I regret doing this, but this pregnancy hasn't been as much fun...I think I want a second bowl of ice cream, any chance you can get me another please?" Norah asked.

"Are you sure the parents of this baby would think you should have another bowl?" Dylan joked.

"Thank you for your concern—but they aren't here right now, so may I please have some more ice cream?" Norah asked playfully. She really didn't want to have to move as it had taken her long enough to get comfortable, but she really wanted a second bowl. She was close to six months along and still had a ways to go. The road ahead was feeling particularly daunting, and she hadn't remembered being this moody during Asher's pregnancy.

When Dylan returned with two bowls of ice cream, Norah smiled. "Thank you," she said. "We can gain the baby weight together."

"Happy to oblige," Dylan said.

Norah loved hiking and continued to hike while she was pregnant. She always saw other people on hikes, and some were very friendly. One day when she was walking, she saw two other pregnant women hiking together. They caught each other's eyes and smiled.

"How far along are you?" one of them asked Norah.

"Thirty-six weeks. You guys?" Norah asked. They were all within three weeks of each other. They continued walking together, talking and comparing notes. They talked about how they were feeling, where they would be delivering their babies, and if they were having a boy or a girl. When the two other women started talking about topics like whether they would be nursing or bottle feeding, Norah wondered how to explain that she would be doing neither.

"Have you thought of possible names for yours?" one of the women asked Norah.

"Actually, this baby isn't mine," Norah said—and the two women looked at her like she just told them she was a convicted felon. Their expressions made Norah feel like they thought she was some impostor who was pretending to be pregnant.

"I'm a surrogate. I'm carrying the baby for a couple," Norah explained. Then just in case that wasn't comforting enough for them, she said, "My husband and I have a son of our own, I just wanted to do this for someone else." Norah noticed their concerned faces soften to curiosity and they continued hiking and asking questions.

The women asked about the surrogacy process. Norah explained that the baby was a boy, and he would come to exist from the forty-seven-year-old's husband's sperm, a twenty-four-year-old donor egg, and her thirty-eight-year-old uterus. The wife wasn't able to have her own child, Norah told them, so this was the next best thing for them. They asked Norah about her son and his experience with the process.

"He has really embraced it all. Given the opportunity, he explains this arrangement to anyone who asks. He is proud of us as a family for being so sharing," Norah said, beaming as she thought about Asher.

With the baby's due date a week away, Norah woke up each morning, looked down at her belly, and smiled at Dylan. "Still pregnant," she said. She wandered around running her errands, making work calls, and doing school runs for Asher, all while knowing that, at any minute, her water could break. As the actual due date came and went, she wondered just how late this baby was going to be. She was ready to give this baby to his intended parents and to be done being pregnant. She told the baby that he better hurry up or he would have to be evicted, but he seemed very cozy. She didn't want to have any medical intervention to start the labor if she didn't have to—but she was running out of patience.

Norah hadn't had any alcohol during the whole pregnancy, but the night before she went into labor, she had a bit of red wine just to relax. She took a long bath and asked Dylan to massage her back because it ached from carrying around this full-term baby. He played masseuse until Norah fell asleep.

Norah awoke at five in the morning to contractions. Finally, the baby was on his way. She woke Dylan up to help her time the contractions, and when they were fewer than five minutes apart, they let the intended parents know. Both couples made their way to the hospital.

Once Norah was checked in, she was already about six centimeters dilated. The transition happened fast—Norah felt the urge to push within a half hour, and after an hour the baby's head was crowning. The baby was born healthy, and the nurse wrapped him up and handed him to his mother.

Norah watched as this man and woman finally realized their wish to become parents. The look on their faces as they stared down at their new son made Norah realize that it was all worth it. Tears flowed from all of them. For the parents, the tears were for all the waiting that had finally come to an end. They had their beautiful baby in their arms. For Norah, the tears came from witnessing that moment, and also from the relief of having reached the finish line. Dylan's tears were from the pride he had for his wife. He held Norah's hand after witnessing all she had done for this couple, and he was in awe of her.

The next day, as she rested in the hospital, exhausted from having the baby, Norah started to feel off. It wasn't because she had a hard time saying goodbye to the baby—seeing them as such a complete family was exactly why she did this. Dylan was home with Asher, so she was on her own. Norah called for a nurse to come, feeling nauseous and woozy. The nurse took her temperature and discovered that she had a fever. The doctor thought she might have a UTI and wanted to monitor her after a day of antibiotics to see if her fever went down. She had to stay in the hospital for two extra days after that due to a reaction she had from the antibiotics.

By the time she felt well enough to be discharged, the new parents and baby were already cleared and sent home. She had given so much of herself to the process that she wasn't sure what she had left. She felt shaken, frail, and so vulnerable. As she sat alone in that hospital room she thought about her home, about Dylan and Asher. She missed being home with them.

In this moment, Norah realized that she didn't want to have another baby of her own. While this thought wasn't an epiphany, she had wondered about her answer before, and she felt certain now. Norah didn't feel an attachment to the baby she gave birth to, but she felt grateful to him for helping her see that she had everyone she needed waiting for her at home.

Chapter Six

Zoey

Right after Sean proposed to Zoey, they started trying to have a baby. She was getting close to thirty-nine, and everyone on both sides of their families shared the opinion that they shouldn't waste time.

"It could take you a while, and you'll want to know what the issues are sooner rather than later," said Zoey's mother. Zoey's period was all over the place, so trying to figure out when she was ovulating would be like guessing a number between one and thirty.

Sean and Zoey both wanted to have a family, but at the same time, they were excited to focus on planning their wedding while they tried. Surprisingly, they got pregnant on the very first try—they were elated, but also cautiously optimistic about the pregnancy. Zoey had a few friends close to her age who had miscarried and she knew it was a likely possibility for her as well.

Zoey had gotten a positive pregnancy test at home but wanted to confirm with her doctor that it was real. She made an appointment and had blood taken, which confirmed that she was actually pregnant. It was too early to see anything on the ultrasound, but Zoey could hardly wait the two weeks until she could bring Sean with her to the doctor to get a look at a heartbeat.

Zoey worked as a restaurant and beverage lawyer. She always loved restaurants, chefs, cooking techniques—anything having to do with food. Her mother was a great cook, and as a child, Zoey enjoyed being in the kitchen with her while she made dinner. She watched her mother perfect her Caesar salads by rubbing garlic on the romaine leaves before adding dressing and parmesan. She appreciated the time her mother took to make sauces and dips and to add the finishing touches to every dish. Zoey's mother was also a great baker and would let Zoey help whenever she made pies or cakes.

As a result, Zoey grew up with an awareness of quality when it came to food, whether cooked at home or at a restaurant. After majoring in political science as an undergraduate, she continued on to law school because it seemed like the obvious next step. When she discovered restaurant and beverage law in her second year, she was driven to combine law with her fascination with all things food.

Sean taught language arts at a middle school—and while their careers seemed incompatible to some people, they were actually well suited for one another. They met at a charity event where several of the restaurants Zoey represented had tables with food samplings. A donation served as an entry ticket, which meant that the event's guests were some of the wealthiest in the Boston area—or, in Sean's case, the friend of a wealthy Bostonian. He wore a crisp pair of dark blue jeans and a tweed jacket with elbow pads, and to Zoey, he seemed out of place in a good sort of way. A mutual friend introduced them, and they talked on and off for the rest of the night, in between Zoey's answering questions about which restaurants she worked with or if she had a favorite. They discovered they shared a love of international food, talking politics, and outrageous comedy.

Zoey had a very specific physical type that she was attracted to—her friends couldn't believe how her ex-boyfriends all shared a similar lanky tall physique and a defined Roman nose. The more pronounced a man's nose was, the more Zoey was attracted to him. When she met Sean, she didn't even consider him romantically. She couldn't identify what his background was. He could have been Latino, Asian, or Native American, but he wasn't tall or skinny, and his nose wasn't big enough for Zoey. Since he wasn't her type, Zoey's guard was down. They spent hours getting to know each other, and Zoey learned that he had an Irish dad and a Filipino mom; he was from Western Massachusetts and still very close with his childhood friends. Sean learned that Zoey was Greek, Jewish, and from Connecticut; she had a few close friends in Boston, but most of her family and friends lived back in Connecticut or in New York. They were both caught off-guard by the intensity of their meeting that night. Both were single and looking to meet someone, but neither was planning on it happening that night.

It wouldn't take long for Zoey to consider Sean romantically. She got past his car being full of yet-to-be-graded papers and that he didn't look anything like Adrian Brody. Suddenly, she started to notice that her feet were being swept off the floor. Sean was taken aback by Zoey's intelligence and sense of humor. She was genuinely interested in his stories about his students, which was rare. In fact, his roommate—who was also his friend from the event—politely explained that Sean's stories from school probably were interesting when Sean was at school, but they just didn't relay well after the fact. Zoey couldn't disagree more.

Zoey and Sean dated for three years, and during that time, they spoke honestly about what they wanted for the future. They shared the same goal of ultimately getting married and starting a family—so when it all happened at once, they embraced it. Neither of them was prone to worrying. They didn't waste time mourning that the order wasn't how they expected, because they had very few expectations to begin with. They just hoped for an outdoor wedding, good weather, loved ones in attendance, and an easy pregnancy.

As they drove to Zoey's first OB appointment, they tried their best to stay calm. They were both excited the day finally arrived, but they felt nervous, too.

"I wonder if the doctor could even hear a heartbeat with mine pounding so loudly as this," Zoey said.

"Mine is pounding too...let's just find a parking spot and take a few breaths. You won't be able to see anything if you pass out," Sean said.

"I just want to get in there already and see something, one way or another. I can't believe it takes nine whole months until you actually get to see a baby on the outside. I don't know how people have patience like that—Sean, can you just drop me off? It's taking forever to find a spot and I don't want to be late." Zoey barked. She was pretty chatty on most days, but on this day, she rambled on nervously.

Whenever Zoey snapped at Sean, he had two relationship superpowers: the ability to not take it personally and to make her laugh when she was upset. "Sure, Zoey, " he said, keeping his eyes on the road. "I can drop you off, and when they ask you to undress from the waist down, you can go ahead and do that—but no one is starting any appointment until I get there. No magic wand is going up your hoo-hah without me." He was matter-of-fact and calm in response to her panic and stayed that way until she started to crack up.

Sean and Zoey went into the appointment together and watched quietly while the doctor explained the screen in front of them. The shadows of grey on the black swirled around like the ocean on a map. They finally saw the developing fetus, as the doctor called it dryly. She then showed them a little movement and turned up the whooshing sounds. She explained that what they were hearing was the heartbeat and that Zoey was about six weeks pregnant. "Wow," Sean said over and over; Zoey smiled, tears of joy trickling down her face.

Zoey celebrated every milestone of her pregnancy. She found it fascinating to see and feel all the changes that came so rapidly over the months. She continued to work, and when she came home from her office, Sean would lie next to her and read to her and the baby. Sometimes, he read the books his students were assigned to read, like *The Outsiders* or *Freak The Mighty*, but as the days passed, he would read anything he could find to Zoey and the baby. Some evenings, he would pick up the newspaper's travel section and try to read the article with an accent from the country being profiled. This nightly ritual got Zoey through some of her more exhausting days. She looked forward to getting home and lying on the bed, just the two and a half of them together.

Sean and Zoey planned their wedding for June when Zoey would be six months pregnant. All was falling into place: Zoey found a dress that highlighted her bump, they found a beautiful garden venue, and Zoey arranged for the event to be catered by some of her favorite clients. As the date approached, the two of them took pleasure in crafting wood-framed chalkboards for the tables, picking out flower arrangements, and taste-testing cake, all while suggesting possible baby names to each other. The excitement and anticipation of all that lay ahead practically had them floating. Their dreams of getting married and having children were coming to fruition, and they were thrilled.

The wedding was beautiful, and they were both so proud to be showing off the baby bump. The weather was perfect, the grounds were gorgeous and everyone they wanted there was able to make it. They looked around and felt so loved by everyone there. At their last doctor's appointment, Zoey and Sean had found out the baby's gender; they decided to tell everyone at the wedding that they would be having a baby girl.

They spent the months following the wedding making a little nursery and taking a birthing class. When Zoey went into labor at home, she figured at first that she was just feeling Braxton Hicks contractions—she'd probably have a few more days. She had just taken off work a week before and expected to have a few weeks to prepare, but the baby came just two days before her due date. The birth was incredible in that it ended up going a lot smoother than they had imagined. There were no hitches, Zoey went from contractions to dilating, to pushing, and for a first-time birth, her doctor was amazed at how quickly it all went. She went into labor at nine in the morning and by noon she was holding her baby girl. After much back and forth between the two of them, Sean and Zoey chose to name the baby Amelia—Millie for short.

In the first few postpartum months, while Zoey had off from work, she and Sean's parents both visited, and Zoey enjoyed showing off their new little girl. When her mom came, Zoey was able to cook with her, and she paid close attention to how her mother did things in the kitchen. She valued these cooking lessons with her mom and committed to cooking more homemade meals now that she had time at home. Once everyone left and she was on her own, Zoey felt like she had enough in her reservoir to do some meal planning. Since she was nursing Millie, she was happy to be eating at home instead of ordering in as much as they had been before Millie was born—this way she could monitor the ingredients she was eating.

Although parenthood took some adjusting to, especially the sleepless nights, it suited Zoey. She was grateful to not have to run to an office each morning and to get what needed to get done around Millie's naps. She had four months of maternity leave and when it neared an end, she realized that she couldn't imagine going back.

Her firm was disappointed when Zoey said she wouldn't be coming back full-time, but together they negotiated working part-time from home. Zoey wasn't thrilled to have to work at all—but she was happy for the opportunity to at least do it while close to Millie: while Zoey didn't want to miss any of Millie's big milestones, she and Sean needed the money. It was hard enough for one person to live on a teacher's salary, let alone three.

Most of the time, Zoey could swing getting her work done with Mille playing or napping, but on the days when it got challenging, she would call a friend or a sitter to help watch Millie for a few hours. This worked until Millie was about two when Zoey found a part-time daycare for Millie a few days a week. Millie was easygoing and adaptable and loved going to preschool and playing with other little kids.

One day while Millie was at daycare, Zoey used the time to go to her annual OB appointment instead of doing work. She was still nursing Millie, so her period hadn't returned. Zoey and Sean had talked about trying again for another baby, but Zoey wasn't in a rush—she was so involved and in love with being with Millie. What other time she had left in her mental bank went to work, Sean, and cooking. She was just getting the hang of her day-to-day and was not sure she was ready to add anything else just yet.

Her doctor surprised her: if they want more children, she advised, they shouldn't wait. Zoey was forty-one, and although she was aware that it wasn't the perfect childbearing age, she thought she had a bit more time. After all, Zoey's doctor told her to start trying as she prepared to get married, and she got pregnant the first time. She went home and told Sean about the appointment; listening to her own voice, she realized that the doctor was probably right. She just wanted to have a second baby on her own terms, when she and Sean felt ready—not when her doctor sent her home with the clichéd "time is running out" message she tells all forty-year-olds.

Zoey wasn't ready to stop nursing Millie but cut down enough to get her cycle back. It never fully regulated—but irregular was normal for Zoey, so she didn't expect a clear road map of when she and Sean should try to get pregnant. They had a few ridiculous nights where they attempted to have sex with Millie sleeping about 5 feet away from them. They were trying so hard to stay quiet so they wouldn't wake her. If she groaned in her sleep, Sean would jump from Zoey as if he was going to scar his little girl. He would whisper towards Millie sleeping as if he was pleading with her.

"If you can just stay asleep and quiet just a little longer, your mommy and I just might make you another little person to play with. Doesn't that sound fun?" Sean asked. Sometimes they went into another room to have sex, and the excitement of being on the couch without a toddler next to them was enough to make them feel like they were on vacation.

After a few months of trying, Zoey got pregnant again. It validated for her that maybe her instincts were right and that it wouldn't be too hard to have another baby after all. This time, Zoey didn't wait to tell her friends or her family. She took a pregnancy test at home and when it came back positive, she started dialing. She had a feeling that she would see the line show up clearly—her boobs were already swollen like they were at the beginning of her first pregnancy.

First, Zoey called her parents and announced that Millie was going to be a big sister. Her parents were thrilled, and Sean was ecstatic—but her friends were hesitant to get too excited. They congratulated her and were happy for her, but they weren't celebrating just yet. Many of them had been in her shoes before.

"Don't you want to wait until you're three months along before you tell people?" her friend Ann asked.

"I would rather share it with the people I am closest to —you guys are the same people I would call if things didn't go well," Zoey responded.

Sean and Zoey drove together to this ultrasound appointment, feeling a lot calmer than they did when she was pregnant with Millie. When they were in the office together, they playfully chatted about how Millie would be with a baby. When the doctor came in, Sean and Zoey were all smiles of anticipation, excited to see the ultrasound. After reviewing the timing with Zoey, the doctor estimated that she was about six weeks along.

"Ok, let's take a look, shall we?" the doctor said, as Sean and Zoey nodded and exchanged eager glances.

The room fell utterly quiet. The absence of any sound from the machine was stifling. The doctor took a breath before speaking, and she seemed to take all of the air left in the room when she did.

"Sadly" was the only word Zoey heard the doctor say. It was the only word she needed to hear her say to understand. It was followed by "There is no heartbeat," but by then Zoey was already spinning. Zoey grabbed Sean's hand and noticed the expression on his face. His eyes were wide, and she could tell he wasn't fully grasping what was happening. This news wasn't something he'd considered a possibility in the same way she had. Zoey had felt a pang that morning, a reminder that she could be disappointed by the appointment, but she'd swallowed back her thoughts—she didn't want to think negatively for no reason. She wanted to say all of this to Sean and just sob in his arms. She wanted to hold him, to soften the blow to his heart, but she was too paralyzed by her own.

As soon as reality set in, the doctor's presence in the room became unwelcome. Their grief was too intimate for a third wheel, and yet the doctor couldn't just walk out. She had to explain to Zoey that she would likely miscarry the baby over the next few weeks and what else Zoey could expect. She explained that Zoey's body would still feel pregnant until she began to bleed and that, if they wanted to try again, they should wait for at least two menstrual cycles. Zoey could process only part of what she was told and figured she could worry about details later.

Later that night, once they arrived home from the appointment, Sean and Zoey did their best to keep it together for Millie. Zoey made her a fried egg, toast, and peas for dinner; that was about all she could come up with, after the day's news. She just wanted to get her to bed so she could fall apart. Zoey told herself she would take the night to feel crappy about it —maybe tomorrow, too—but she wanted to look ahead after that. Tons of women have miscarriages early on, then get pregnant again and have healthy babies. It's common, and Zoey was trying to remind herself of that, but it wasn't making her feel any better.

At bedtime, Sean read Millie *Knuffle Bunny*, their nightly ritual. Occasionally, Millie would request the second or the third books in the series, and most nights Sean would oblige and read all the voices. When Trixie went boneless in the story, Millie would reenact a tantrum while Sean pretended to pick her up. Tonight, Zoey watched her little family. She thought about joining Millie on the floor and lying boneless—if she could muster up the energy to move. She hoped to be able to add to her family, but for the moment she focused on what was in front of her. She looked up Mo Willems, the author of *Knuffle Bunny*, on her phone and learned that Trixie was the name of his daughter. There was no mention of another child.

Zoey wondered if that was a choice or if their family had also gone through what she was experiencing.

Millie did not fall asleep easily—sleep wasn't something that she ever needed the way that other children did. Napping caused way too much stress to even try to enforce, and bedtime required Sean or Zoey to lie down next to her. Zoey took the position that night and curled up next to Millie. She pulled her in, tucking Millie's head right under her chin. She inhaled, reaching her face into the top of Millie's head smelling the combination of shampoo and Play-Doh. She couldn't seem to get close enough to her. Zoey had tears in her eyes as she hugged her child to sleep. It took what seemed like a miracle that every cell came together in just the right order, that every organ grew to function, and that every muscle grew in just the right place. Zoey was not a religious person, but she held Millie and thought *this is what it feels like to be blessed.*

Zoey and Sean did get pregnant again—and each time, between six and eight weeks, she would miscarry. Over and over again, she remained hopeful that maybe this would be the one that worked. She tried acupuncture, changed her diet, and exercised, but still kept miscarrying. With each loss, she felt more determined. She had less and less enthusiasm for work but found herself needing to create. She went to work in the kitchen, baking and cooking. She opened recipe books that had only decorated her shelves in the past. She baked desserts and wrapped them in pretty paper bags to give as gifts to friends. Sautés, stews, cakes, cookies, pasta, pastries—from bourekas to bagels, she made it all. Having a plan in front of her, being able to follow it, and watching its execution come to pass each time gave her a sense of completion and accomplishment.

Sean and Millie reaped the benefits of Zoey's new obsession with cooking. She loved taking care of her family, and it satisfied her to see them both enjoying her food. As her cooking increased, her desire to sit at her computer to work decreased. She did the bare minimum, fighting herself to put down her kitchen projects every time there was a work project to do.

After her sixth or seventh miscarriage, Zoey lost count of them. Sean and Zoey never went to her doctor without the anticipation of getting bad news. They both carried themselves in as if they were wearing life jackets, ready to keep their heads from sinking. They, especially Zoey, knew that there would not only be a possibility of miscarrying again, but a likelihood. When she asked why the answer the doctor would say that the likely reason was her age. Every time Zoey heard or read another piece of information about how a woman was most fertile in her twenties, she grew angry. Her research showed that when a woman is over thirty-five, her chances of producing a healthy egg with all twenty-three chromosomes is only one in four, and Zoey, given her age, would be thirty-five percent more likely to miscarry than younger women. After learning more, Zoey kept seeing the number thirty-five everywhere she looked. Pregnant women seemed to surround her, and she resented them walking around, smugly cradling their baby bumps. There was a fine line between jealousy and envy that Zoey tiptoed after losing so many babies.

Zoey felt tense and upset all the time, and she grew tired of feeling so down. She talked to Sean about leaving her job. They did the math, wondering if they could make it work for a little bit. Zoey wanted to go to culinary school and eventually start her own catering company. She had all of the contacts she would need and a full understanding of how to build a successful business. Sean was supportive of Zoey —if she found joy in cooking, he knew she needed to chase this dream. They were both ready to exit the roundabout of trying to have another baby. Any new outlet was a good option. He was relieved to see her passionate about something other than fertility. As much as he wanted another child, he wanted his wife back more. He was ready to let the idea of having another baby go in exchange for her laughing again, or even just smiling again.

Zoey gave notice at work and signed up for the professional culinary program at Cambridge School of Culinary Arts that very same day. Millie started preschool full-time; after dropping her off in the morning, Zoey went off to class herself. She poured herself into every ounce of learning she could acquire. She refocused on the fundamentals, the history of world cuisines, science, techniques, and skills. She learned about spices and seasoning, about unique and exotic flavors, and how to incorporate them into recipes. She absorbed it all like a lady finger drinking up the espresso when making tiramisu. Culinary school gave her the sense of adventure, excitement, and newness that she was looking for.

When Zoey completed the classes, she invited her and Sean's parents and Sean's to join her, Sean, and Millie for a feast. Zoey wanted to celebrate. She wouldn't have news to share of another pregnancy, but she did want to share all that was cooking in her oven. From all of the heartbreak and disappointment that turned to focus and dedication, Salty Baby Catering was born. It was a long labor and not an easy delivery—and it took some time to find the support it needed—but then the business, and Zoey, thrived.

Chapter Seven

Diana

There's a muscle memory that kicks in when you walk into a place you haven't been in years. The curve of the walls, the turn your body makes subconsciously in the right direction, the memory of sounds and smells, the dog's claws tap-dancing across the hardwood floor, garlic sizzling in a pan.

Diana hadn't been to her parents' house since her parents were there together on her last visit. When her father had passed away a few days before, she couldn't catch her breath. He was almost eighty and had a heart attack. He had been getting older and had all kinds of aches and pains, but overall, he had no major health concerns. Diana flew in from Atlanta to Connecticut, where she grew up. Her brother Brett would be meeting her there the next day, but Diana wasn't sure she could make it a whole day without Brett there with her. She didn't know how the house could feel exactly the same when everything had changed.

For the past two-and-a-half years, it seemed that trying to have a baby was all she and her husband Scot could think about. Diana had had six miscarriages, three of them with complications—she never successfully made it into the second trimester without losing the baby. They spent thousands of dollars on fertility treatments, only to come out of it with empty arms and empty wallets. They went through a failed adoption that, in hindsight, seemed like a scam. They tried to use a surrogate, but that fell through in the eleventh hour. Diana was ready to wave her white flag. It seemed everything in the world of motherhood was against welcoming her in.

Scot owned a restaurant in Atlanta, and that was *his* baby. He and Diana both wanted a child, but with every failed attempt, he poured himself back into the restaurant. Diana didn't have that same escape. Her mind and body endured so much with each unsuccessful attempt. She suffered from endometriosis, meaning the tissue that usually grows inside the uterus grows outside, causing intense pain, heavy periods, and fertility issues. Every month she got her period was literally a painful reminder that she wasn't pregnant. The times when she had gotten pregnant successfully, she dealt with being exhausted, cramping, and ultimately miscarrying. Diana was a third-grade teacher, so there was no escaping being around children while she tried not to focus on her inability to conceive.

Scot convinced Diana to give her body a rest and to restart the process of adoption. He researched reputable agencies in an effort to prevent the mess they had gotten into the first time. They were in the early stages of investigating the different options that adoption sometimes offered, like choosing the child's age, race, or gender. Scot and Diana were a mixed-race couple; Scot was African-American, and Diana was white. They had always pictured themselves as parents to a couple of little mixed-raced babies. They hoped that, if they couldn't have their own, at least they could adopt a child of color to start their family.

Diana was doing her best to ignore her desire to give birth, but she wasn't succeeding. She and Scot did enjoy being able to go back to a sex life that didn't revolve around tracking the ovulation days, trying the best upside-down positions to lie in afterward, or looking at failed pregnancy tests. Diana was able to stop that part of her brain, but she wasn't able to stop seeing babies everywhere she went.

When Diana got the call about her father, she was on her way home from teaching. Her brother called her and by the tone in his voice, she knew whatever he had to tell her was serious.

"Diana, are you driving?" he asked.

"Yes—are you okay?"

"You have to pull the car over, Diana. Pull over and tell me when you've stopped," Brett instructed.

"I'm off to the side—please tell me what's going on." Diana's heart raced in anticipation of whatever news Brett was about to share. She braced herself.

"Dad died, Diana. He had a heart attack, and by the time he got to the hospital, he wasn't breathing."

Brett said the words articulately enough for Diana to hear, but she could tell he was crying. Brett was two years older than her, and they had always been close—he always looked out for Diana, and he wished he could protect her from this pain.

Diana and her dad were very close. They talked every few days. No amount of bracing herself had prepared her for what Brett had told her. She thought that he was going to tell her that one of their parents was sick—she feared hearing the words "cancer or stroke." She thought that, if one of her parents suffered from a heart attack, it would be a tough time, she would take time off to go home to care for them, and then they would get better, leaving them bonded together and grateful to come out the other side.

How could it be that the sky was still as blue as it was before she answered Brett's call? How would she ever be able to turn her car back on and drive? His words slayed her, and when they finally landed in her brain, she exploded in wails.

Scot had to meet Diana where her car was parked. She was exhausted from crying, and he didn't want her to drive home so upset. He held her that night as she tried to understand how her life would work without her father in it. She felt pulled between her own sadness and concern for her mother. She spoke with her mom on the phone, but they were both too upset to say much. Diana reassured her that she would fly in as soon as she could, and her mother reassured Diana that she would let friends stay by her side until Diana got there. Scot offered to fly home with her, but Diana knew he couldn't leave the restaurant that long, and she would need him to help her get through the funeral once they planned it.

Diana's legs trembled as she walked around her family home. She reached her mother, and they collapsed into each other. For the two of them, embracing one another was the closest they could feel to Diana's dad. They made their way to the couch to sit down, rested their heads on each other's shoulders, and interlaced their fingers together. They sat silently, holding each other, as neither one had known where to begin to lift the weight of sadness. Diana knew that once Brett joined them the next day, they would start talking about what needed to be done, but she and her mother just sat. It was impossible for them to ignore the emptiness in the room that had once been filled by the man they both loved so much.

Brett arrived, snapping everyone into a forward-moving direction. He took moments to mourn with his mother and sister, but he also faced the reality that they needed to plan a funeral. He kept Diana on-task, and she was grateful to have a clear plan of assignments. That night, after a long day of making all the arrangements, the three of them sat down to eat some Thai food that Brett picked up.

"Dad would have loved that we're all sitting here together," Brett said

"Yeah—but he wouldn't be a fan of your choice of Thai dishes," Diana said.

It was the first time they smiled in what felt like weeks, but it had only been a few days. Brett loved red curry and his dad was never a fan, but Brett always insisted on ordering it. Their dad always predicted that Brett would order it and announced when the bag arrived that he would bet $100 that there was red curry in the bag, so having Diana bring it up made everyone smile. It was the first of many new firsts that would be shared without their dad, but at that moment, they took a first step together to face their new reality with some humor. It was a welcome shift.

Scot flew in for the funeral, and Diana didn't realize how much she had missed him until she was in his arms. Diana's dad was the first of either of their parents to pass, and as she hugged Scot tightly, she thought about how they would have to go through this three more times together. Suddenly she remembered their attempts to have a child, and it dawned on her that, if she ever did become a mother, her father would never meet his grandchild. When she let her thoughts flood out loud to Scot, he nodded his head, locked eyes with hers, and said "I know, and I'm so sorry."

After the funeral, the out-of-town guests started saying their goodbyes and the house grew quieter again. Buster, the family dog, began following Diana around. She appreciated his company: Buster used to follow her dad around like that too, and Diana knew that she and Buster both missed him so much.

Scot needed to go back to Atlanta to the restaurant, and Diana decided to take some time off of teaching to stay with her mother for a few weeks. As part of her new rituals, Diana started taking long walks with Buster each morning. When she got back, she and her mother would have breakfast and decide what they needed to check off their lists that day. They sent thank-you cards to guests, canceled all of her dad's credit cards, transferred his bank account information, and completed other tedious tasks that were both boring and sad simultaneously. Each day, they would plan a treat for themselves in the afternoon, like going to town to browse the shops or stopping for ice cream. Diana went with her mother to her water aerobics classes, a buffer for anyone who hadn't yet found out that her father had died. Diana's mom wasn't sure she was ready to be social, but with Diana by her side, she felt stronger.

One morning, while Diana was out with Buster, Scot called her phone four times. She didn't bring her cell out on walks with her—the reception wasn't great, and she found it peaceful to be alone with Buster and the trees. When she came back and saw how many calls she had missed from Scot, she felt a pang of fear. She wasn't quite over the shock from Brett's phone call about their dad. She tried to catch her breath as she rang Scot back.

"Diana, where were you, did you get my message? What do you think?" Scot asked. He had excitement in his voice, so Diana exhaled and relaxed her body. Whatever he had to say wasn't bad news.

"I was out on a walk with Buster. I didn't get to listen yet, I called you back first."

"We got chosen to adopt through the agency we registered with. The birth mother is six months along. We could be getting a baby, Diana. Finally!" Scot said.

"What else do you know about her? I'm surprised it happened so soon after we registered with them...I am afraid to get too excited." Diana confessed.

"I know, babe, but I have a good feeling about this, and guess what? The baby will be mixed-race. The mother is white, and the father is Black, just like us." Scot said.

Diana felt herself reaching for somewhere to sit. The last few weeks had been such a whirlwind that she hadn't thought about the possibility of a baby. She had lost so much—but here was the potential for a new life to enter hers, and the possibility overwhelmed her. She and Scot wanted this for so long, and now that a real opportunity had presented itself, she was afraid to let herself be happy. She had spent so much time in sadness—but maybe her father was somehow part of this gift. Diana wasn't an overly religious person, but she prayed to her father at that moment, to tell him that she was grateful for him and for the possibility of this new baby.

Diana shared the good news with her mother and Brett. The idea of a baby was a bit of good news they needed after such a sad month. Diana decided she would leave a few weeks later to head home to Atlanta to be with Scot, but before she did, she set up a plan for her mother. Together they set up a daily, weekly, and monthly plan that included meal prep for one, books that she and Diana could read together while they were apart, social plans with close friends, and daily exercise. Diana promised never to leave without a plan for when they would see each other again, so they promised Diana to come back a few months later.

Scot and Diana chose Atlanta as their home after they got married for a few reasons. The food scene there was just beginning to buzz after being known solely for southern fare; the city was ready for some new types of cuisine. Scot found a great spot to open a restaurant and found willing investors. Diana was ready for a change and had no trouble finding a teaching position in an elementary school in Atlanta, hoping to start a family soon after getting settled. Atlanta also had a diverse population, one that was very accepting of interracial couples. They had lived in a few other places where they didn't always have the most welcoming experiences. Atlanta was not perfect, but they decided it was a good start.

Scot and Diana were each always pretty open about race and the idea of being with someone from a different one. They had both been raised in a diverse upbringing, but having friends from a different race, they both found out, is different than being in a relationship with someone from a different race. When they first introduced each other to their families, they received a range of responses, both positive and negative. Diana's parents had always been very liberal and had a large diverse group of friends. Diana knew they would be accepting of Scot right away—but she wasn't expecting the talk from her father once he knew they were serious. He sat them both down and told them that being married to each other would not be easy. Marriage is challenging, he said, and being an interracial couple would add to their challenges. His intentions were to help prepare them for the realities of racism, but Scot and Diana were caught off guard—they had been hoping for congratulations.

Diana's father had explained that interracial relationships had made strides since he was young, but that systems hadn't changed enough—and if people don't continue to fight to make systemic changes, the progress made will mean nothing. He told Diana that Scot will always be at risk and that there will be times he will not be safe, as well as times when the two of them being out together won't be safe.

Both Scot and Diana came to appreciate her father's words over time. They weren't ignorant of the prejudices that would come their way, but race didn't define them as a couple. They had been pulled over, traveled at the airport, checked into hotels, and always gotten the same looks or comments: the looks that say "Are you two together?" or comments that prove not everyone in the world is ready to accept them as the unit they are—or the family they wanted to be.

Scot's family also took a long time to warm up to the idea of Diana. Scot's mother had met a few of his girlfriends in the past, who had been African-American, so she was surprised to learn that the woman he was most serious about was white. Although she never said it outright, Scot's mom hinted that there were plenty of Black women that were available. Before anyone in his family would get to know Diana, they had to get over her not being Black.

All of this factored into their conversations about having a child, and it became apparent to both of them that, if they could not conceive their own child, then they would go out of their way to adopt one that resembled both of them or was African-American. As much as they wanted the world to be as open to interracial relationships as they were, they knew that if they adopted a white baby, Scot might encounter problems when he was out with his child without Diana. As horrible of a reality as that might be for them to accept, they didn't want their children to have to deal with extra hardships. They knew that they would always face some affliction surrounding identity—so whatever Scot and Diana could do to keep it minimal, they would do.

Diana arrived back home to Atlanta in time to meet the birth mother. Amy was a twenty-one-year-old college student with hopes of getting her graduate degree.

She and her boyfriend found out that she was pregnant and decided together that the baby would be put up for adoption. Neither Amy nor her boyfriend felt that they were at a stage in their lives where they could emotionally or financially provide what the baby would need. Amy had registered with the same adoption agency as Diana and Scot because the agency made explicit their support of transracial adoptions. Amy chose Scot and Diana immediately after reading about them. Amy had hoped to keep the adoption open, in that she wanted photos occasionally to show her that the baby was doing well. Other than that, she didn't request any involvement in the child's life.

Amy was nearly seven months along when she met Diana and Scott. The pregnancy had gone smoothly, and Scot and Diana were able to go to most of the remaining doctor's appointments with her. They all became friendly, but Diana and Scot stayed slightly guarded. They hoped that Amy wouldn't change her mind as her due date grew closer. They had been close to adopting before and knew that not getting to bring the baby home was always a painful possibility.

Diana slowly allowed herself to daydream about the idea of becoming a mother, with tempered optimism. This could finally be happening—and although she hadn't bought any baby gear, she was gathering ideas of what they might need when they became parents. She went from watching new mothers with envy to watching them with curiosity. She looked at their strollers, baby carriers, and cute baby clothes and imagined what it would be like to have some of these things for a baby of her own.

Scot came home one Saturday night after work and surprised Diana with a little box. Inside was a delicate gold necklace with the word "Mama" imprinted on a thin flat gold bar.

"I couldn't wait until tomorrow to give it to you," he said. "I know we aren't there yet, but we are so close, and I wanted you to have it for Mother's Day tomorrow."

"Thank you, Scot," Diana said as her eyes welled up. "I love it—but I am so afraid to let myself believe this is actually going to happen."

"I know, babe, but we have to plan as if it will and deal with whatever happens later," Scot said. "We better get moving on some stuff because Amy is due next month, and we don't even have a car seat to take the baby home with."

With Scot's encouragement and positivity, Diana let herself prepare for bringing home a baby. She let friends know that they were expecting a baby, and many of them offered hand-me-downs, which Diana graciously accepted. With all the offers that came in from friends to share their baby gear, Diana and Scot were only left with a few items that they still needed to get. While Scot was at the restaurant one day, she spent hours cleaning out their guest room/office to make it a nursery. After such a productive afternoon, Diana was exhausted and laid down to take a little nap. When she woke up later to see Scot resting next to her, she realized a few hours must have passed.

The next day, Diana started to ponder why she felt so tired the day before. She wondered if she could be pregnant but knew the likelihood of that possibility was slim. She checked her calendar to see when her last period was and saw that she was a few days late. She dug quickly through her bathroom drawers searching for a pregnancy test, then remembered that she had gotten rid of every pregnancy-related item in the whole house after her last miscarriage. Diana tried to rationalize her desire to run to the closest store for a pregnancy test. She had been in this place before—and even if she was pregnant, she had never gone past nine weeks. Most importantly, she was about to become a mother in a matter of weeks.

Diana's curiosity got the best of her; before she said anything to Scot, she wanted to know for herself. She bought a pregnancy test, stuck it in her purse, declined the cashier's offer for a bag, and ran from the store as if she might get caught pursuing this false hope.

When she got home and took the test, it was positive. She couldn't wait for Scot to get home later on and called him at the restaurant.

"I'm pregnant, Scot."

"What? What are we going to do?" Scot responded in a panic.

"What do you mean what are we going to do? We are going to adopt our baby and wait and see what happens with this pregnancy," Diana said.

"What do we do if we end up with two babies? That's crazy!" said Scot.

"We can't return one just because another one might come—and if we did, then we could end up with no babies," said Diana.

The questionable "what if" factor in their equation stumped them both. There was the chance that Amy could have the baby and decide to keep it after giving birth. There was the chance that the adoption could work out and they could become parents to a newborn. There was *also* the chance that Diana could miscarry again—or the possibility that she wouldn't. They could have two babies, one baby, or no baby. They just had to keep moving forward and wait and see.

Diana went to see her OB and explained the past few months: her dad dying, the adoption, and the pregnancy. The doctor responded matter-of-factly.

"You do have quite a lot going on. I'm sorry about your father," the doctor said, and although Diana knew he was being genuine, she could feel how uncomfortable it was for him, not knowing how to react to everything Diana had told him. There was an awkward beat because neither of them quite knew how to segue out of the conversation.

"Let's do some blood work and an exam and see what's going on," the doctor said, and Diana was grateful to have him return to his regular businesslike tone.

Diana didn't have Scot come to the appointment with her, since she knew nothing conclusive would come from it. When her doctor began her ultrasound, Diana stared up at the ceiling. With each second that passed, Diana prepared herself to shift her focus back to gratitude. She and Scot were about to adopt a baby. She reminded herself that she had already wrapped her mind around not having her own biological baby. The moment she held their new baby, the journey of how the baby got there and how they became parents wouldn't matter as much. The time that had been taken up for so long with getting to someday hold a baby would be filled with parenting her new child.

Before Diana could even crane her neck to look at the monitor, she heard a heartbeat.

"There is the heart." Diana's doctor moved his finger around the monitor as he pointed out what he saw. "There is the head, the spine, the legs, and the arms. Based on the size of the fetus, you are about nine weeks along."

This was shocking news to Diana—she had only ever been this far along once before. She locked her eyes on the tiny figure on the monitor, trying to memorize every detail. If this pregnancy, like all the others, didn't last, she wanted to marvel at what was actually happening at that moment on the screen. She was pregnant and had created a tiny little person. If she couldn't celebrate having her own baby one day, she chose to celebrate what she saw before her.

Her doctor printed out the slick strip of three black-and-white ultrasound photos. Diana thanked him, looking down at the shiny, curling thermal paper in her hand, and tried to find the ground to place her feet down. It all felt surreal, familiar, and yet so outlandish.

The doctor told Diana to come back in three weeks and to take her prenatal vitamins and folic acid before sending her on her way. She wondered if she would make it back to that appointment in three weeks and still be pregnant, or if this was the last time he would see her as a pregnant patient. Diana knew what it was like to sit hopefully in the waiting room hoping for more ultrasound photos. She also knew what it was like to sit there in pain, watching women with bigger bellies come out with pictures while she waited to have a D&C.

Diana drove straight to the restaurant from the appointment. She watched Scot while sitting parked in her car. He was lighting all the little faux tea lights on the tables, preparing for the dinner rush. She knew the news she was bringing would transpose the trajectory of their adoption plans. She watched him, thinking about the life they created together, and how—with all of the curve balls the last year had thrown at them—they were able to catch, handle, and deal with them together. Diana was relieved the restaurant was fairly empty as she walked up to Scot. He was surprised and happy to see her, as he loved when she stopped by on his long workdays. She hugged him and, without saying a word, handed him the ultrasound pictures.

"Nine weeks," Diana said. Scot looked at the photos and then back at Diana, smiling. He felt a wave of joy wash down his whole body.

"This is our baby?" Scot asked, without lifting his eyes from the ultrasound.

"Yes, but..." Diana started to explain that the chance of miscarriage was still high, but Scot interrupted her.

"Let's just see what happens. We've got a lot to look forward to, and there is no way to predict how this will all play out."

So many cells need to align within the perfect timing, in the perfect order, to have a healthy baby. Forty-six chromosomes, countless nerves that grow within the skeletal system, and millions of neurons all have to come together in a wondrous way. When Diana thought about the process, it became astonishing to her that so many healthy babies even existed. Putting pregnancy into perspective helped Diana submit to her concerns and let nature take its course. She focused on preparing for Amy to give birth.

Diana and Scot accompanied Amy to her last doctor's appointment before her due date. Diana had not shared with anyone other than Scot that she was pregnant—she was early enough in the pregnancy that she wasn't showing at all yet. In comparison, Amy's belly looked like she was carrying a watermelon under her shirt. It felt peculiar for Diana to sit next to Amy and the other pregnant women in the waiting room. While they kept their hands on their bellies, Diana kept hold of her secret. Once inside the examination room, the doctor showed Scot, Diana, and Amy the baby's measurements. She explained that Amy could go into labor at any point soon, and it was time to make their arrangements for birth.

As they left the appointment together, the three of them made a plan for how Amy would contact them when she went into labor.

"How are you feeling, Amy? Is there anything you need that we could help out with?" Diana asked.

Diana was not only completely grateful to Amy for choosing them to be the parents of her baby; but she was also in awe of how strong Amy was.

"I'm a little nervous about how the birth will go, but it will go how it goes, I guess. No backing out now," Amy said

"We will be there if you need us. We don't want to be in the way, so we're hoping we can help however is best. If you want us out of the room, in the room, at the store buying you junk food, you just let us know," Scot said.

Amy's last appointment was a week before her due date, so when Diana and Scot said goodbye to her that afternoon, they knew it might not be long before they would meet her at the hospital. As the days grew closer, Diana grew anxious about Amy changing her mind. She thought about how hard it would be to let go of a baby after carrying it for an entire pregnancy. She wondered what life would become when she wasn't waiting for a baby. The only time she *hadn't* thought about becoming a mother in the last few years was when she was drowning in sadness from losing her dad; although it was nice to have a reprieve from wanting, the desire had been replaced by so much grief. She had been living for so long on tenterhooks. She struggled at this final stretch, which would determine their fate as a family.

Diana had her own OB appointment later that same week; this time, she asked Scot to come along with her. No matter the outcome of the appointment, they wanted to be together. As Diana sat in the waiting room, her fingers interlaced with Scot's, she took inventory of how many times she had occupied a seat in this waiting room before, anticipating the news delivered within the exam room. She took in some deep breaths and slowly counted as she exhaled. There was nothing she could do that would change the outcome of their situation, so she tried to keep herself as present as possible.

"What are you thinking about right now?" Diana asked Scot. She was desperate to get out of her own head.

"That I would have designed this room in a much nicer way than they did," Scot said playfully. "There is much better art out there than what is hanging here."

It wasn't exactly what Diana was hoping to hear—but it worked. She started to look at the art—all flowers—and couldn't be sure if they were real paintings or just cheap prints. She wondered why flowers were so often hanging in obstetricians' waiting rooms. She figured that photos of babies would be too upsetting to women like her who had trouble actually making one. Were the flowers meant to be a metaphor for life? If they were, then Diana thought it was a poor choice—flowers don't live very long. Or could they be a symbol of the vagina, a knockoff version of a Georgia O'Keeffe? She'd noticed that flowers were hanging in Amy's doctor's office as well and wondered if some course in medical school instructed students to hang flowers in waiting rooms when they got licensed. Scot squeezed her hand.

"Your head is going. Hey, look at me for a second," Scot said.

Diana turned her face to his and looked deeply into his eyes, his eyes that over and over again have been a comfort to her. "We got this. No matter what, it's all good."

"You started it when you brought my attention to the bad artwork. Now all I am doing is staring at them and wondering if they meant to put flowered vaginas on the wall," Diana said.

"Now I need to stare at it for a minute too, hold on," Scot said smiling.

Once inside the room, Scot got quiet. They had rubbed off on each other and Diana's mood had lightened. She was ready to get the appointment over with, and Scot's humor in the waiting room helped her stay distracted. Scot had been able to shelve any concerns he had until they sat in the room. Diana changed out of her pants and underwear and hopped on the table, quickly draping a paper skirt over her waist. She knew at any time there would be a knock at the door followed by the doctor just opening it. The knock always caught her off-guard, so she sat on the table tilted towards the door to be ready.

After the doctor greeted them, he quickly shifted to the checkup and began their ultrasound. Diana reminded herself to breathe as the doctor navigated the ultrasound wand. Scot had his hand on Diana's shoulder, watching the monitor. The swooshing sound was loud enough for both Scot and Diana to hear, but they glanced between the doctor and the monitor to confirm what they were hearing.

"There is your baby." The doctor outlined the figure on the monitor with his hand pointing out, head-to-toe, a tiny human. "Nice strong heartbeat—and, based on these measurements, you are about twelve weeks and two days along." He was pleased for them, knowing how long they had tried in the past.

Diana stared at the screen as if looking away might change what she was seeing. She had never gotten this far along in pregnancy, and she knew that—although there were never any guarantees—she was out of the first trimester, a great sign. She looked over her shoulder at Scot and saw that he was glowing. His smile was radiant, and Diana felt the warmth of his joy wrap around her. She kissed his hand that had been resting on her shoulder, and he reached down and kissed her head.

"Wow" was all Scott could manage to say. They scheduled the next appointment for three weeks later, and Diana felt like she had finally been invited into the club of patients that goes for regular pregnancy appointments. It wasn't until they reached their car that they finally said anything to each other.

"We are having a baby," Scot said.

"Actually, we are probably having two babies," said Diana.

"Holy shit!" said Scot.

Diana and Scot decided to keep the news of her pregnancy quiet for a bit longer—they didn't want anything to interfere with the adoption finalizing. They also wanted to treasure the news to themselves.

Scot and Diana tried to wrap their minds around the idea that their lives would go from being just the two of them to growing into a family of four. Diana let her principal know that she was in the process of adopting, but she would have to take more time off than she planned if there were two babies coming. She and Scot had quite a bit to figure out—but they felt like their problems were good ones to have.

Just three days after Diana's doctor appointment, Amy called to say that her contractions started and that she would head to the hospital when they were five minutes apart. Diana and Scot cleared the rest of their day so that, when Amy told them she was on the way to the hospital, they could meet her there. Amy hadn't found out the gender of the baby, so Scot and Diana decided to find out along with her when the baby was born. All Diana and Scot had hoped for was a healthy baby—the gender wasn't important to them. They had also decided together that they didn't want to attach themselves to the idea of who this baby would be until it was theirs. They hadn't landed on any one name yet for a boy or a girl but instead had a short list of a few they liked.

Amy's labor started late morning and she didn't start pushing until after ten that night, but once the baby's head started to crown and Amy began pushing, her delivery moved quickly. Amy went to the hospital on her own; she felt that her baby was always meant for Diana and Scot, and bringing her boyfriend or a friend with her to the birth might foster more curiosity about the baby. She wanted to be able to focus on the birth, get Scot and Diana the baby safely, and then return to school. Amy was a swimmer, and when she started pushing, her athleticism was apparent. She was focused and determined as she reset between pushes. It didn't take many pushes before the baby seemed to shoot out.

Diana and Scot watched in awe as the doctor swiftly pulled the baby up and placed it on Amy's chest. One of the nurses asked them both if they wanted to cut the cord together, and as they leaned in close enough to see the baby, they saw that it was a boy. A son! Amy looked at the baby and smiled as Diana and Scot marveled over him. Once he was cleaned up, he was placed into Diana's arms as Scot took him in. Amy was exhausted but even in her post-delivery haze, she remained supportive, honest, and straightforward about the adoption. She never strayed from her objective of seeing Scot and Diana become the parents to her child.

Once Amy was strong enough to leave the hospital, she signed all the necessary paperwork to finalize the adoption. Scot and Diana decided on a name for their baby boy before they left the hospital with him: Kyle Brandon. Kyle after Diana's dad, who was named Karl, and Brandon because they both always liked the name.

When they brought Kyle home from the hospital, Diana was three months pregnant with his little sibling. As Kyle doubled in size, Diana's belly grew right along with him. Six months after Kyle was born, Diana went into labor. Her mother was visiting so that she could watch Kyle while she and Scot headed to the hospital. As her contractions got closer and closer they marveled that they were soon to be a family of four. They were grateful to have witnessed Amy's delivery to Kyle as it helped give them an idea of what to expect. After a few hours of contractions and then a few more hours of pushing, Diana gave birth to a healthy baby girl. Diana and Scot named her Adeline Ray, or "Addie" for short.

Kyle and Addie filled their home with spirit and vitality in all the ways Diana and Scot had hoped that having a family would. They kept in touch with Amy and every Mother's Day, Diana thanked her for being Kyle's first mother—and such a generous one, at that. Amy was thrilled that Kyle had a baby sister to grow up with and requested pictures of both children from time to time. Once a year, they all got together, and Amy developed into a fun, aunt-like friend that both kids adored.

The timing of the order of events that led Diana to finally become a mother was not lost on her. She got pregnant right around the time her father passed away, and Scot told her of the possibility of adopting Kyle right after she lost her dad. Just as one of the most important people in Diana's life faded away, two beautiful new souls came into it. Even if it was clichéd, Diana couldn't help but wonder if her father had worked miracles for her. After all, it had been looking like there might not be a baby in the cards for Diana and Scot—and then the wonder of wonders happened, and they ended up with *two* miracles. The perfect remedy for losing her father was for Diana to look at the new family she gained.

Chapter Eight

Asako

Asako had lived in Japan her whole life and had never traveled far from her hometown until she moved to Tokyo to study nursing. After she graduated, she got a job working at a university hospital as a nurse. There, she met Kevin, who was working as a translator at the hospital. Kevin was an American from the Midwest who had studied Japanese in high school and was taken with the language. He'd moved to Japan after college and taken a job at the hospital while trying to build his career as a graphic artist. A mutual friend had encouraged them to meet, but Asako was very shy and spoke no English— although she noticed this fair-haired American in the hospital, she didn't know what they would talk about.

Their friend couldn't wait for them to meet by chance, so she made it happen on her own: she invited them both out to lunch together during a workday. Kevin could speak Japanese well enough, but he was clumsy when trying to find the right words. Despite their language gap, they connected and began dating. A little after a year later, they moved in together.

Kevin felt at home in Japan, and his career was beginning to gain traction. He left the hospital and got a job with Focus, a big design firm in Tokyo. For two years, he and Asako lived in Tokyo and enjoyed city life by going out with friends, exploring new parts of the city that neither of them had seen, and trying out new restaurants. Kevin asked Asako to marry him, and she said yes; they were married in her hometown in Japan.

As newlyweds, they had planned to stay in Japan, but an opportunity for Kevin arose in America that he couldn't refuse. He was limited in Japan, and advancement at his firm seemed dependent on not only his years of employment but also his language skills. Leaving Japan was a difficult, layered decision that impacted each of them differently. Kevin had planned on living in Japan ever since high school. He spent eight months of college in Kyoto, moved to Tokyo after graduation, and worked hard to build a life in Japan. He knew that the position offered to him in America with a Japanese firm was better than any offer he could get from that same firm in Japan. Being bilingual was an asset to his company, and taking this offer could mean that he and Asako could eventually move back, or at least travel easily between countries.

For Asako, leaving Japan meant leaving everyone and everything she had ever known. She spoke no English and had no idea what living in America would be like. She was excited about the adventure, but also terrified—she loved Kevin and wanted to be by his side to support him. Although this was a new chapter, Asako tried to view the experience with an open mind, the way Kevin had imagined Japan when he moved there for the first time.

Kevin and Asako moved to San Francisco; they found an apartment, and the week after they moved in, Kevin began his new job. He worked long hours and felt overwhelmed in the beginning, adjusting to his new position and finding his way within the company. While he was at work, Asako tried to learn about this new city and country. She felt deeply alone, but she went out every day in an effort to find her footing. She found a Japanese group for people who had recently relocated to San Francisco, and through that, she found a part-time accounting job that she could do without needing to speak English. She became friendly with a few women in the group and, although she was terribly homesick, just being able to speak to someone from Japan was comforting.

Kevin was also trying to acclimate to life in San Francisco. Even though he had lived in Tokyo, he had never lived in a big U.S. city. Coming from the Midwest, the culture, the pace, and the traffic of his new city were so different. He was Catholic and felt a great deal more at peace once he found a church. He explained to Asako that the same sense of home she felt from being able to speak Japanese and be understood was the same feeling he felt at church. Asako wasn't Catholic, but she understood exactly what he meant. Despite the many differences between the way Kevin and Asako were raised, each of them respected the other immensely. They were both experiencing so much change, yet they had a shared way of handling each situation as it came to them without jumping too far ahead. This measured temperament served them well during the uncertainty of their first few years in San Francisco.

Asako and Kevin both wanted to have children, but they wanted to wait until they were more settled in their new life, both financially and mentally, before bringing a new life to their family. About three years after moving to America, they started thinking about having children. Asako was a healthy, fit thirty-five-year-old—so when she didn't get pregnant on the first few tries, she didn't worry. After six months of infertility, though, she grew concerned, and pregnancy became all she focused on. She checked for her ovulation, counted the days of her cycle, and had sex with Kevin on the days before she could be ovulating, the day she thought she was, and the day after to increase their odds. Two weeks after trying, she would take a pregnancy test; when it inevitably wasn't positive, she would wait for her period so that she could begin the next month's attempts. Trying to conceive turned making love into a reminder of what *wasn't* working.

Living in San Francisco had finally become more familiar to Kevin and Asako, but infertility wore heavy on them, creating some disconnection. Asako, after three years of living in the city, felt lonelier than ever. One day, when visiting friends from her Japanese group, she confided in one of them that she and Kevin were struggling with infertility. Her friend shared that she had gone through a similar struggle and gave her the name of a fertility doctor. Asako went home and mentioned it to Kevin that night, who agreed that they should meet with him.

At their first appointment, the doctor explained that, since they had been trying to get pregnant for six months without conceiving, Asako was considered eligible to start treatment. The doctor suggested they try intrauterine insemination, known as IUI, as a first step. Kevin and Asako tried to take in everything the doctor was telling them, but the information was arriving quicker than they could process. They left the appointment optimistic that there were options, but they wanted to learn more about what IUI actually was.

The next day Asako reached out to her friend who had referred her to the doctor, and she was kind enough to explain all of the details in Japanese about how IUI worked. Asako then explained the procedure to Kevin. While they both wished that they could conceive on their own, they agreed that it was time to get help.

The next month, Kevin and Asako tried their first round of IUI and waited hopefully the two weeks after the procedure, for the first time not handling it alone. When Asako took a pregnancy test and learned she wasn't pregnant, she was disappointed, but not discouraged. With the support of their doctor, they looked ahead to the next month and tried again.

Month after month, Kevin and Asako tried IUI without success. After six months of trying IUI without resulting in a pregnancy, doctors recommend moving on to in-vitro fertilization, or IVF. When Kevin heard about the process, he needed time to consider it. Asako, who was prepared for this possibility, had already done her research on the procedure. She worked with numbers for her job—and with every month that passed that she wasn't pregnant, she kept tallying the months, maybe years, it could take until she would have a child.

As a religious Catholic, Kevin worried that IVF would be frowned upon by the Catholic Church. He was concerned that an embryo created in a lab would not be considered a natural way to procreate within Catholicism. He did some research and found that the church might not approve of IVF: when multiple embryos are created and frozen, there is a strong chance that some of them won't be used. The unused embryos, after being frozen, are likely then destroyed—and since the church believes that life begins at conception, this presented a big moral dilemma for Kevin.

Since they were in San Francisco, the Catholic church Kevin attended was a bit more on the liberal side. Asako was aware that he was struggling with the decision to attempt IVF, so—despite feeling impatient with their infertility—she supported his path to find a solution that felt comfortable to both of them. Kevin decided to speak to the priest directly, despite feeling so afraid of what he could say. He knew he and Asako were ready to become parents and needed some help to make that happen.

"God will not judge you for wanting to become a family," said Father Edward. Those were the first words that fell over Kevin like a warm blanket. He had been so concerned that he would get advice from his priest to reconsider medical treatment for infertility. Instead, he was met with kindness and understanding that he and Asako had been struggling. Father Edward didn't say explicitly that he condoned fertility treatments, but he expressed an understanding that times are changing and that Kevin and Asako's devotion to each other and to God would guide them in the decisions that faced them. Kevin went home that night to Asako with a sense of calm.

"Let's give it a try," he said.

"Are you sure you are okay with it, Kevin?" Asako asked.

"Yes," Kevin said.

The next day, Asako called the fertility clinic and asked about the next steps to begin IVF treatment. She and Kevin made an appointment to receive the medications required to stimulate Asako's egg production. She needed nightly injections that Kevin helped her to administer. After a week, it was hard to find a spot that wasn't hard, bruised, or red from the previous injections. Kevin didn't like having to hurt his wife with the jab of a needle each night, but she was taking it all in stride, keeping her eyes on the goal.

To complete a round of IVF, the doctor extracted eggs from Asako and had Kevin contribute a sperm collection that same day. Next, the doctor united the egg and sperm in the lab to create an embryo. Meanwhile, Asako had to start another medication to prepare her uterus's lining to receive the embryo. After three days, Asako returned to the clinic so that the doctor could implant the fertilized embryos, inserting them via a catheter into her uterus. The doctor explained that he got three healthy-looking embryos from the fertilization and wanted to implant two of them. Once the procedure was over Asako went home to rest. After two weeks, she took a pregnancy test. She was not pregnant.

When they returned for treatment, the doctor's response was not at all kind or comforting. After all Kevin and Asako had gone through, he seemed dismissive, barely answering their questions. After all the time, money, and heartbreak they'd experienced, Asako and Kevin were hoping for some kindness—not someone who made them feel worse when they got bad news. Asako was becoming disheartened, and Kevin reassured her: that they were doing everything they could and that they should persevere. They both reached out to people that they knew and cast their nets a little further, hoping to find a new doctor. Asako was a very private, shy person, as was Kevin. Speaking up about their struggle to become parents was not easy for them, but the stakes were high. For the first time, they did not feel alone—because from that moment on they took every step of the rest of their journey together with a few friends that they felt safe sharing their experience with.

Kevin and Asako found a new doctor with a much softer bedside manner, and with this doctor's help, they began the IVF process anew. They weren't positive that they would be able to become pregnant, but they at least felt confident that they had found the right professional to help them keep trying.

Within two months of working together, Asako and Kevin got the news that they had been waiting for—they were pregnant. The moment they heard, they were speechless. Asako began to cry; she immediately tried to tell herself not to get *too* excited. Even if she miscarried, she was happy to hear that she was able to get pregnant. They had been waiting over two years for this news.

"I hope they are calling us and have the right information—that they didn't give us somebody else's good news," Asako said in Japanese through her tears to Kevin.

"I'm not worried about that. I think it is just hard for us to believe it is finally happening," Kevin said. Asako placed her hands on her flat belly as if discovering it for the first time. She looked down at her hands, gently rubbing them around to welcome this new little being to grow inside her. She then looked up at Kevin, smiling.

"I'm so happy," she said.

"This is great news," he replied as he kissed her forehead.

For the next few weeks, Asako rested. She had gotten this far to get pregnant and wanted to do everything she could to help *stay* pregnant. When she was six weeks along, she and Kevin went in for the first ultrasound, They saw a beautiful, tiny beginning of a baby and heard it's loud, strong heartbeat. They were both thrilled, relieved, and in awe. To them, they saw the combination of science and God create a miracle—and they were grateful to both.

Asako's pregnancy continued, but it wasn't uneventful. She retained excess water early on and swelled larger and larger as the pregnancy continued. She had to buy all new clothes and shoes so that she could have things to wear that fit. One day, her skin began to itch, and Asako thought she might have irritation from something she had eaten. The small patch on her arm didn't go away the next day—instead, it grew to cover her whole arm.

Over a week's time, Asako's whole upper body became red and splotchy, and it itched something awful. She went to the doctor, who explained to her that what she was experiencing was called PUPPP, which stood for pruritic urticarial papules, and plaques of pregnancy and that it was a common pregnancy-related skin condition. Sadly, there was no cure, but her doctor suggested peppermint oil or oatmeal baths to soothe the itching. She tried both treatments, alongside a few other gentle solutions, but she felt so uncomfortable. She wore her clothes inside out so the seams, tags, and fabrics wouldn't irritate her that much. She tried cold showers, warm baths, ice packs, and heating pads, but the itching remained throughout the remainder of her pregnancy.

Asako did not want to complain, and she did not take for granted that she was experiencing all of these issues because she was going to have a baby. She was *actually pregnant*—that fact kept her smiling. Kevin felt for Asako and saw how much she was enduring. He offered her some of her favorite foods, gave her foot massages, and helped with errands so she could rest.

A few days before her due date, Asako's water broke. She didn't yet have steady contractions, but when Kevin called the doctor, he suggested they go to the hospital. When they arrived, Asako was examined to see if she was dilated at all. The baby was monitored, and once the team saw that all was okay, they told Kevin and Asako to stay in the hospital and walk around to help labor progress.

After two hours, Asako was checked again—nothing had changed. They gave her some pitocin to move things along and used a Foley balloon to help dilate her cervix. When her contractions finally began, they arrived close together and strong. She received an epidural for pain, but she could still feel the intensity of the tightening of her contractions.

When she was instructed to push, Asako grew excited that she could meet their baby soon—but within a few pushes, the room's tone changed rapidly. The baby was in distress, with a sped-up heartbeat. The doctor made eye contact with Asako and Kevin and calmly said "We are going to move into an operating room and do a cesarean section so that we can get your baby out safe and sound." It wasn't what Asako had hoped for, but she trusted that she was in the right hands.

Asako could hear a lot of noise and movement around her. She heard them say something about needing to push the baby back up. She looked at the ceiling, surrendering to what was happening around her. She was no longer being asked to push or to take deep breaths—she didn't have to do anything but stay positive, wait, and hope that everything would go well. Because of the epidural, Asako could not move from her waist down. She moved her head so she could see Kevin, and she met his concerned eyes, locked in on him, and smiled. She had no energy to find words, but she knew things were going to be alright, and she wanted him to know that he didn't have to worry.

Kevin had been resting his hand on the operating table near Asako's upper body. Asako moved her head so that Kevin could cup her head in his hand. They stayed like this as Asako felt the tugging and pulling happening below the paper medical curtain. She felt a great deal of pressure, and then a weight being lifted—she looked up as the doctor hoisted their baby above the curtain. She saw Kevin smiling, and together, they heard the baby begin to cry.

"It's a girl!" the doctor said, and the joy they'd waited so long for rushed in.

Asako and Kevin took turns holding their baby and staring at her. They looked at her mouth, nose, eyes, and ears, marveling at how amazing it was to have her finally here with them. It truly did feel like a hard-won miracle that every cell had come together in just the right way to make a healthy baby. They decided to name their baby Kiko, which meant hope in Japanese; it suited her immediately.

Kiko made Asako and Kevin a family. They took pleasure in the privilege of being her parents, full of wonder as they witnessed every milestone she met. Their hearts expanded into a reservoir of love they didn't even know could exist. Shortly after Kiko's first birthday, Asako and Kevin began to talk about having another baby. They weren't sure how long it would take, or how much help they would need, so they wanted to plan ahead. They decided to try on their own first and were shocked when Asako became pregnant right away on her own. When Kiko was two years and two months old, she received a baby brother named Ena. Kevin and Asako were no longer searching. When they looked at their family, Kevin felt closer to God, and Asako finally felt at home.

Chapter Nine

Grace

B rooklyn, is the most densely populated county in the state of New York coming in second to Manhattan, the most densely populated county in the U.S. Brooklyn has a rich mix of cultures and history. It is home to Orthodox Jews, Puerto Ricans, Polish, and Dominican residents. Williamsburg is an area right over the bridge from Manhattan that used to be inexpensive until the little-known secret of its low rents for large artist spaces spread right over the bridge to Mahnatinites desperate for more space. In the late 90's Williamsburg was beginning its gentrification and slowly becoming known for its art scene and hipster culture. New York City taxi cabs before then would not even drive over the bridge to Brooklyn, but soon enough that was where everyone wanted to go.

Williamsburg was attractive to anyone moving to New York City in the early 2000s. It was cheap and had lots of cool places to go out, lots of parks, and lots of other transplants from all over the rest of the country. Myles had moved there from Ohio a few years before Grace had moved to Brooklyn. She had further to travel, and it took time to shed so much of her Texas upbringing before she found herself in Williamsburg. Grace had friends from home who got out before her to welcome her to New York when she arrived. She was a visual artist with some work lined up for herself in the city. She got an apartment with a friend from Texas and slowly over time built her life in New York. She didn't want to date anyone in the beginning. She still had ties back home she needed to sever. As her months went on in New York the idea of returning to anything or anyone back in Texas became less feasible to Grace. She fell in love with Brooklyn.

Grace's friend Vanessa wanted her to meet Myles. She knew Grace wasn't interested in getting involved with anyone but she wanted them to meet since they had so much in common. There were quite a few times when they were both in the same place but just didn't happen to meet. Or they met and something got in the way of them both being able to talk to each other for more than a couple of minutes, like the time Grace and her roommate had a party and both toilets overflowed. That night Myles just gave up and went home. When they both finally did start talking to each other it was hard for them to stop. Vanessa was right. They both had so much they connected on.

Myles was interested in Grace and wanted to be exclusive right away. Grace was not at all ready for that and explained that she was very much dating other people. They did not take off right away. They went back and forth for a few years before the timing was right for the both of them. When they finally went in, they went all in and were quickly inseparable. They moved in together and soon after announced they were getting married. They both knew they wanted to have a family so they didn't even wait for the wedding to start trying for a baby. When Grace didn't get pregnant right away she didn't think much of it since she knew it could take some time. She set her sights on the wedding and getting their families together for the big day.

Grace and Myles had a beautiful wedding in Big Sur. It wasn't the big wedding they had both originally imagined. The venue they had planned for in Brooklyn ended up closing down causing them to pivot and change their idea of the kind of wedding they wanted. They were told Big Sur was beautiful and took a trip out to see it. When they took one look they knew they wanted to get married there. They gathered together with the most important people in their lives and vowed to one another that they would hold each other's hands through all of life's moments to come. They went back to Brooklyn happily as a husband and wife.

In the time it took Myles and Grace to settle in as a couple, it seemed like all their friends had gotten married and started having babies. Grace had even thrown a few baby showers for a few of her close friends. By the time her third friend told her she was pregnant, Grace had been trying for a few months. She had been skilled at putting on a smile for her friend's news, but her ability to feel excited for other people's pregnancies was proving to be difficult. It wasn't like she wasn't happy for them, it was just that she wanted to be experiencing pregnancy too.

Grace had heard stories of the great lengths that people had gone through to get pregnant. She had decided that she wouldn't spend crazy amounts of money, put herself through frozen embryo transfers, timed injections, or waste months of her life focused on procreating. If it didn't work out eventually she would adopt. She had already done some research on adoption and Myles was on the same page with her.

Grace went to her OB and told her how long she had been trying and asked for advice on what to do next. Her doctor suggested they try Clomid. The medication helps stimulate egg production resulting in increasing her chances of getting pregnant. Grace gave it a try and after a few months of that not working they moved on to the next option. IUI, Invtrauterine insemination. This process was getting less romantic and more expensive very quickly. IUI required a sperm sample that goes through a process to leave only the most viable, and that sample is then put into a catheter which is then extended vaginally up to the uterus where it is released. The hope is that by placing the sperm right near where the egg will be they will meet, connect, hang out, and then do what they are supposed to do, make an embryo. When IUI didn't work for them either, Myles and Grace learned that the only way that pregnancy would be possible was through In Vitro Fertilization, they had to decide what measures they were willing to take.

Grace had to rethink why she said she would never do IVF. Was it because she didn't want to put her body through all of the hormones? Was it because it created this lifestyle that practically took every ounce of your energy causing an obsession with just trying to get pregnant? Was it because she wasn't sure they could afford it? Did she think it made pregnancy any less natural because science stepped into help? Did she think maybe they could go through all of these efforts and maybe it still wouldn't work? Did she think it meant that her body was damaged in some ways and wished she could just fix it? Yes was her answer to all of these questions she had swimming around in her head, but if this was the only way for them to experience making a baby then the answer to trying it was also yes.

Insurance covered more of the cost of the fertility treatments than they expected, but it was still wild to hear how much it would cost them. Grace and Myles agreed that they would only try for a limited amount of time and that they had a limited amount of funds. They knew going into this that it would require them to have a level of patience, faith, and strength. It was a nearly impossible headspace to get into because your complete focus and dedication had to be turned toward conceiving a baby, yet you were simultaneously not supposed to get attached to the idea of getting pregnant. They were supposed to remain positive even though disappointment seemed to be an inevitable component.

The first step of IVF required Grace to get her ovaries in the right shape to increase the number of eggs. This is done by suppressing the hormones to prevent premature ovulation. Meaning she was pumped full of hormones. She had to do injections and go in for daily bloodwork to monitor her levels. Then about two weeks later Grace had to have an internal sonogram (which was not at all pleasant) for hormone assessments to measure follicle size, and once that was achieved she had to have an injection for the final maturation of the eggs, and all of this was just the beginning. These hormone injections made her feel off. She was moody, but also a bit crazy. She was grateful because she had heard for some women it made them feel like they were losing their minds.

The second step was egg retrieval which has to be done three days after the last injection. She had to be sedated, which she felt was the best sleep she had gotten during that whole process. The retrieval was done through an IV and an endocrinologist using a needle guided through a vaginal ultrasound was used to guide the way to her eggs. Once the eggs are retrieved they are put into a special formula and incubated until insemination. Once she woke they were able to tell her how many viable eggs they got.

The third step is fertilization and done by the doctors at their lab. They used the best eggs from Grace and the strongest sperm from Myles and put them together. This step allowed Grace some alone time to rest up and also focus on something other than being poked and prodded since she knew that there would be more of that to come. A few days later they got a call to say how many eggs were fertilized and were growing. They are checked for viability and then they have to set a date for transfer.

The next step is a transfer which compared to the prior steps seemed physically a lot easier. They just implanted the two most viable embryos and then they waited, and waited, and waited. To think some people just had sex and that was all it took. It was difficult for Grace to imagine how easily pregnancy came for others. She would walk down the street and see pregnant women and wonder how they got there. Was it easy for them, or did it take trying a while? She tried not to be bitter, but it was hard to see people everywhere around her just having babies. Would she ever be able to join them? She wondered what was wrong with her that she couldn't just get pregnant, she also judged herself for every negative thought she had towards others around her that could.

The waiting was brutal and yet oddly also a pacifying time because she knew that she and Myles were doing every single possible thing they could do. She felt like this route that they were taking left them with actual chances of working. She accepted that as much as she wanted to do it the natural way, science could make something possible for them that was seeming otherwise impossible. After two positive blood tests showing that Grace's hormone levels indicated pregnancy, they went to the IVF clinic for an ultrasound which confirmed they were indeed pregnant. The ultrasound also confirmed that there were two babies with two very strong heartbeats. Grace and Myles squeezed each other's hands and watched the monitor in awe. This was finally happening. Two tiny humans were growing, and they were theirs. They said little to each other as they left the appointment, but their smiles said enough. They each called their families from the street to share the good news.

Grace was walking around New York City keeping her lips sealed. She had this most exciting secret that she thought about practically every second but she couldn't tell anyone. She and Myles waited the obligatory twelve weeks before sharing her news with anyone other than immediate family. Once she made it through the first trimester she told everyone she could think of. She had a few friends who were pregnant at that same time, and she was so excited to join them to experience this wonder all together.

Myles had suggested they get the genetic tests done for the babies to screen for any chromosomal abnormalities or diseases. Grace did the testing and when they got the call letting them know that both babies were healthy, she let out a big sigh of relief. They were having a boy and a girl. This was happening, they were going to be a family of four. They were both elated. After every hurdle and hoop they jumped through, IVF had worked for them. With the combination of love, science, and a lot of persistence Grace was pregnant with two little people.

Grace and Myles enjoyed the process of planning and playing house. They looked at pictures of baby furniture for a nursery and threw out different names for the babies. Grace spent a lot of time with her pregnant friends chatting about different birthing methods and ideas of how they would get their babies home from the hospital. Cab rides meant no car seats, but subways were too crowded for a new baby. They shared laughing fits about their stomach sizes, stretch marks, and stories of their most ridiculous cravings. Grace's cravings were the most cliche because she had to have a pickle first thing every morning. They compared notes on the research they had all done on baby products until they had each narrowed down the lists enough to pick their favorite strollers, bouncy chairs, and gliders.

The first purchase Grace and Myles made for themselves was a glider. When the package arrived at their apartment Myles took it out of the box and assembled it in record time. He wanted to surprise Grace when she got home from work. When she walked in the door and saw it, she looked back and forth between Myles's eyes and the chair. Just seeing it sitting there made the room ready for a baby. It made this far-off possibility that they had been waiting for a reality. Grace dropped her bags, took off her coat, and sat down in the chair. Myles looked on as she glided back and forth, floating.

As the weeks went on and as Grace's belly grew bigger, she prepared their lives to accommodate their soon-to-be son and daughter. With every doctor visit, flutter of kicks, or episode of heartburn, Grace's identity was morphing into that of a mother. The moment she woke up in the morning she reached down to greet her two little ones growing inside her, and when she went to bed, she drifted off to sleep wondering about who they would be.

Grace was working in midtown and would take the subway from Brooklyn each day to her office. She was not the most comfortable carrying around her new heavy front load, but she loved finding comfortable maternity clothes that also showed off her growing belly. She enjoyed going into the office and having her officemates comment on the progress of her pregnancy. Unlike her friends who knew exactly what she was going through, her office mates were curiously excited for her and had many questions. "Do you miss drinking?" Ted, her office mate asked. Ted was in his late forties, gay, and lived with his long-term partner. They had no kids, except for their two cats, and one dog, and that was enough family for them. Ted said he was happy to be an uncle but that he never aspired to have his own kids. He was always checking in on Grace, and she appreciated his random questions.

"Honestly, I don't miss having a drink. I barely like eating these days, but I do hope after these guys come out I will want to again."

Ted offered to buy her a drink when that day came around because, in his book, she earned it. She was often uncomfortable trying to sit at her desk and had to get up frequently to move around and stretch. Her boss, Layla was nice enough but she was all business. She never engaged in any conversation with Grace about her pregnancy, but she didn't ignore it either. She just matter-of-factly asked Grace when she was due, when she would be out of the office, and for how long she would take off from work. Other than that there was no small talk about anything other than work.

At fifteen weeks along, Grace felt a tightening and releasing of her muscles around her belly. She knew the dangers of going online and looking up questions, so she called her doctor right away. She was relieved to learn that false labor, also known as Braxton Hicks contractions can be felt earlier in the pregnancy when you are carrying twins. The doctor reassured her that it was okay and to take it easy when she started feeling tightness.

At nineteen weeks along Grace was at work, went to use the restroom and when she looked down she noticed some blood. It wasn't heavily flowing out of her but she also wasn't just spotting. She called the doctor who instructed her that it was probably nothing major but to head over to the nearest hospital just to be checked. When she was finally seen she was told very matter-of-factly that her cervix was opening, and they set her up on a bed with her legs lifted at an angle so that they were higher than her heart. They explained that this was called the Trendelenberg position. As if lying with your head lower than your legs would physically prevent the babies from moving down. Grace waited legs up with limited information for Myles to make his way to midtown Manhattan to meet her. She had called him in a panic and he did his best to get to her without trying to panic himself.

After what felt like hours of waiting Grace was seen again by the OB on call. He explained to her that when a cervix opens too soon a procedure called a cerclage can be done that allows the cervix to be closed with a few stitches to prevent preterm labor. He was considering it for Grace but told her that in her case her uterus was already too exposed and that she would be at risk for infection, and other complications. This is when Grace began to feel his words only sporadically entering her consciousness.

Grace was admitted to the hospital and Myles spent as much time by her side as they would let him. Her nurse told her that she just needed to get to twenty-eight weeks, and if she could do that the babies would be able to make it. Grace responded to her that she was aiming for thirty. The hope was that her positioning and medication would help prevent any more labor. She would have to stay in the hospital for the duration of her pregnancy on bed rest. Her doctor visited the next day and was on board with this plan. That was a Friday, and with the news of what had happened Grace's mother and sister flew out to see her. It was nice to have them by her side but Grace sent her sister home after the weekend because she had small children, and because Grace thought she would be in the hospital for the next two months. Her mom stayed by her side past the weekend and would remain there until Grace got seen again. She didn't want to leave until she knew her baby would be okay.

Grace was not okay though. The doctor on call who checked her Monday seemed emotionless given the weight of the words that came from his mouth. He explained that her cervix had continued to open. She was doing her best to understand the pieces of the process that she would have to go through. Since the cerclage wouldn't work there would be no safe way to keep her babies growing inside her, and preterm labor would be inevitable. She had just felt them moving shortly before he said this, so she could not fathom that they were at risk. How was it that there wasn't something to be done that could help her?

The next day, a Tuesday, Grace went into labor. Much to her dismay her body was going into giving birth mode. Just shy of twenty weeks along, eight weeks too early, her contractions began one after another. With her mother and Myles by her side, Grace was wheeled into the delivery room. The enthusiasm and encouragement that would surround you when you gave birth was something that Grace had looked forward to. She hadn't spent much time thinking about what it would be like for her when she would finally have the chance to be in the delivery room, but she knew that this was not at all the way she imagined.

The delivery room was somber and it was clear going in there would be nothing celebratory when they came out. There was the doctor and two nurses with them. Everyone was matter-of-fact and quiet at the same time. It was understood that this was a difficult situation but when they quieted their voices they also seemed to diminish their niceties too. Without the excitement of giving birth, the whole process seemed like the most invasive medical procedure ever, without the finish line Grace was hoping for. "Bring your hips down a bit more, bear down, and push for two three four" were the words Grace heard but not in the tone that sounded right. The doctor pulled what looked like a small bundle from between Grace's legs as she tried to blink tears away to see. The nurses seemed to be blocking her view and trying to distract her from seeing what they saw.

"Is that my baby?" She asked. Can I please see the baby?" she cried. Her doctor came over to Grace, Myles, and her mother but didn't seem able to make eye contact with Grace. The advice from the doctor was that Grace shouldn't hold the babies because they are not full-term so it might be too difficult to process. Myles knew his wife well enough to know that there was no way she would leave that room without seeing her babies. He told them to please bring the baby over. Begrudgingly the doctor walked away and instructed the nurse to let Grace hold her baby. It was a girl, and she was so tiny but she was also fully developed and beautiful. Immediately Grace was so glad she didn't take the doctor's advice. She knew she wouldn't be able to hold her baby forever but she was in no rush to give her back. Despite the difficult reality that this little girl would never grow, Grace took pride in what she had worked so hard to make. While her baby was in her arms she and Myles decided to name her Wren. They never chose any definite names for either baby, but Wren was on their list and it meant small songbird. Within the deep sadness that consumed Grace, she held her little Wren in her arms while making a mental picture of her before she disappeared forever.

Wren was born at noon, and a few hours later Grace began laboring again. Her baby boy was born at five and no amount of practice from earlier in the day made this birth any easier. The doctor and nurses knew enough to not try and sway her from holding her son. They wrapped him up and placed him in Grace's arms. The name Grace and Myles chose for their son was Theodore, which meant a gift, and he was. Theodore was just as perfect as his sister with ten fingers, ten tiny toes, a beautiful mouth, and a nose. Grace cried more than she thought one person ever could in one day, but she also kept blinking back her tears to allow her eyes to take in her babies before they were taken away.

Eventually, she had to hand Theodore back just as she had done with Wren. Grace was not prepared to say goodbye to her children before ever getting to know them. This was never on her radar as a possible scenario and she was not only devastated but also upset with the way everyone around her seemed to be lacking in knowing what to say. Every cell of her being seemed like it turned on her. Her body was responding to having just given birth without the awareness that her babies didn't survive. Her mind was racing with disappointment, shock, and anger. Her heart was heavy with the depth of sadness from which she couldn't see ever being able to rise above.

Her identity had shifted in just one day. She went from a mother-to-be to one that never got to set sail. She fell into her own mother's arms and let her hold her. Her mother kept repeating "I'm so sorry Grace. I'm so sorry." Like Grace, Myles and his mother-in-law's eyes were swollen from crying. There was no handbook for this and no clear next steps. Much sooner than any of them expected Grace was released from the hospital. She wondered what she had to go home to and how she would put one foot in front of the other.

Somehow the world around her kept turning, but Grace just didn't feel part of it. Myles had the forward thinking to gift the rocking chair to one of their expecting friends. He knew coming home and seeing it there would be painful, but seeing it not there stung almost as badly. That night they composed an email together that they would send out to let friends and family know what had happened. Within an hour after sending it Grace's phone was buzzing with texts, and emails were coming in with responses. It was clear right away that no one knew what to say, and even if they did, none of it would make her feel better. She knew people were just trying to be thoughtful and kind, but despite the messages coming in, she felt more alone.

Her closest friends, the ones she would normally pick up the phone to talk to with any other life crises were all pregnant. She wasn't sure she could see or speak to any of them. She was no longer in the club she had waited desperately to get into. Grace took a few weeks off of work, she couldn't fathom the idea of being around anyone and needed some time to let her body and mind process this loss. She wanted to go to bed and wake up when it was all over, but what did being over even mean? She suddenly wasn't a mother-to-be anymore, and if the new life that she had ahead of her wasn't going to come to fruition then who was she? She wondered where she fit.

People proved again and again that they did not know how to respond to a kind of loss like hers. As if the experience itself wasn't trying enough, dealing with the logistics afterward was salt on her wounds. Myles and Grace had decided to have the babies cremated and when they talked to the person doing their paperwork he told them he would give them a two-for-one deal because the babies were so small. She knew he was trying to give them some sort of break, but she was so upset at this man for not realizing how dismissive it was to her babies. Just when Grace thought everyone she knew had been informed of their loss someone else would call and ask her how her pregnancy was going. It was an endless amount of uncomfortable interactions.

A few weeks after being home, Myles had convinced Grace to go to a support group. He wasn't thrilled about going either but they needed to do something to try to heal. Sitting together in a circle with other couples who had also experienced the loss of a child was something that they thought might make them feel more understood. They had hoped to feel more connected to people, but in the end, it made them more connected to each other. It was a heavy circle of feelings with people talking about how God had a plan, or heaven just got a new angel. They talked about their hopes for "sunshine or rainbow babies" the ones that come after a loss. There was a lot of deep sighing and nodding in agreement with what the other participants had said. It wasn't that Myles and Grace didn't understand what the rest of the group was feeling, they just didn't understand how they were all dealing with it with such magical thinking. They left feeling that at least they were in agreement that going back to the group wasn't for them.

At six weeks post-pardon Grace had to return to her OB's office for a check-up. She did not want to step foot back in the office. It was hard enough for her to walk past pregnant women on the street but to sit next to them in a waiting room was unbearable. Grace tried her best to avoid anything and anyone related to child-rearing. She had so much anger and resentment around not being one of those women having a regular pregnancy appointment. Her name finally got called and she went into an exam room glad to be sitting on her own. She was sitting in the gown that was left for her to change in, just wanting to get this whole appointment done with when the nurse came in.

"How is breastfeeding going?" The nurse asked ignorantly.

"Well, it's kind of hard to nurse dead babies," Grace responded without hesitation.

How can everyone be so clueless as to handle a situation like this? She was at her doctor's office. If any place should have notes on her file on what a horrible experience she had been through, shouldn't it be her doctor's office? The nurse's eyes widened and she ran out of the room without saying anything. Grace never saw her again and that was fine with her. Her doctor's bedside manners were an improvement from the nurse, but not by much. Grace was reeling and stopped hearing half of what was said to her there. She just wanted to get home.

Eventually, Grace went back to work because it would probably be the best distraction. On her first day back most people darted their eyes at her nervously not knowing what to say. She didn't want to talk to anyone anyway so it worked out for her to just put her head into her work projects. Not long after Ted walked over to her desk. She was glad to see his friendly face after so long. He leaned over her desk looked right into her eyes, took a deep breath, and then let out a big sigh. He didn't have to say a single word but between his sigh and his expression, he conveyed that he was sorry for everything she had gone through. Ted knew nothing he could say could make her feel better and was acknowledging how much the whole situation sucked. Grace appreciated Ted's gesture and for the first time felt seen by someone other than Myles or her family.

Once Grace's cycle had returned to regular for a few months Myles brought up the idea of trying again. When Grace had been pregnant with the twins Myles had the opportunity to switch to a different insurance company that would cover two more rounds of IVF. Grace didn't think they would ever need IVF again since she was pregnant at the time, but Myles decided to make the change just in case. It turned out to be a good choice. Grace couldn't image putting any part of herself through the IVF process again, but she knew she wasn't ready to give up on trying to have a baby. They went to a new fertility specialist and reluctantly Grace began taking all the medications and doing daily hormone shots to prepare herself once again. During the first cycle that she had done with the new clinic, they had over-suppressed her, meaning there were too many eggs. She was instructed to wait another month before trying again, but also told to not have any sex because she was producing so many eggs. It was yet another delay in her efforts to become a mother. The next month she tried another cycle again. This cycle resulted in a healthy embryo which was implanted into Grace's uterus.

Grace and Myles got the news that they were pregnant once again. Although two embryos were implanted only one of them came to be. Grace had decided to switch to a high-risk doctor for this pregnancy. She had been given the option when she was pregnant with the twins, but she wanted so badly then to believe that all was going to be fine so she chose to stay with her regular OB. It was one regret she felt most responsible for. When she met her new doctor for the first time she was asked many questions about the details of her past pregnancy. Immediately, Grace knew she was in better hands based on this woman's responses to Grace's experience. She expressed how she would have handled Grace's situation differently and the pregnancy that both Grace and the babies went through put all of them at risk. She didn't deliver this information in a snarky way, but rather just explained her reasoning for why she would have done things differently. She explained that keeping Grace's legs up above her heart was dangerous and an old-school way of thinking because it was proven ineffective. She also explained that had Grace come to her when she was pregnant the first time she couldn't say that what happened to her wouldn't have happened. There were no guarantees but she would be happy to work with her to try again.

There was a clear plan in place for this pregnancy and for the first time in months, Grace sensed a bit of hope. The doctor said that she wouldn't have had two embryos implanted again given Grace's history. Grace did not allow herself to believe or accept that she was having a baby, but she did feel in good hands during this last-ditch effort. The doctor wanted to see her every week from week eight to twelve, then at twelve weeks they would do the Cerclage procedure to try to prevent any early labor. She would need to be off her feet for three hours every day from week twelve to week twenty and then she would go on complete bed rest. She would be allowed to shower every other day and then go to her appointment with the doctor every Wednesday. She lived for Wednesdays to get to hear a heartbeat and see the baby move. For a few weeks, the appointments were every other week and the waiting seemed unbearable.

When Grace got to the nineteenth week, the same week that she had lost her twins, she braced herself. She told herself this time would be different with different doctors, different precautions, and a different plan. One night, one week later when Myles was out at a work event, she was home alone and felt a contraction. It was way too early and way too similar to the timing of her last pregnancy. She tried not to panic, but within that hour she had three more contractions. She went to the hospital and this time her high-risk doctor met her there quickly. She was monitored and then released cautiously. From that point on her doctor wanted to see her every week again.

At twenty-seven weeks Grace's doctor measured her cervix and she determined that it would be best for Grace to be admitted to the hospital. She would need medication to keep her uterus calm as well as monitoring both morning and night.

Although she wasn't happy to move into the hospital for so long, she felt like this new system and routine left little room for error. She packed as many comforts from home as she could fit into her bag.

She tried to make her new room as cozy as possible while also trying to keep her outlook optimistic.

Her hospital roommates didn't inspire her to stay positive. One was an orthodox Jewish woman who believed in "G-d's law" so much that Grace had to turn the lights on and off for her on the sabbath since electricity was against her belief for that one day a week. Grace wondered if this woman prayed enough did she think it could save her baby? Didn't she realize that even strict prayer couldn't guarantee her a healthy baby?

Her next roommate was there because she had severe gestational diabetes. She was on a strict diet with no sugar, but when no one was looking she would sneak down to the vending machine for bags of Skittles. This woman already had multiple kids at home and her doctors had an exact scientifically proven plan that could help her have another healthy baby and she chose not to follow it. Grace resented her for being so careless. Every time her blood was tested and her sugar levels were up so high she would shrug innocently as if it was out of her control.

The weeks in the hospital were long and monotonous but Grace was stable and for that she was grateful. Myles came to her with lunch every day since there was only so much hospital food she could stomach. As her pregnancy bump continued to grow so did her confidence. She and Myles allowed themselves to talk about this happening. When she got passed week thirty she could practically see that finish line ahead of her. Five weeks later, in the thirty-fifth week, she went into labor.

On the morning her labor started, Grace called her parents and sister to tell them the baby was coming. They were able to catch the next flight available to New York and made it to the hospital in the early evening. This was a long-awaited day that Grace was never sure would come. Even though it was happening, she still didn't trust that it would end successfully. True to the rest of their journey getting to the prize of holding their child, the birth wasn't without complication. A nurse gave Grace too much pain medication while she was in labor causing her to pass out. Once she was revived and felt the urge to push it wasn't long after that her baby was born. At that exact moment, the oxygen mask she had been wearing had slipped up by her ear making a loud whirring sound that was preventing her from hearing anything else. While everyone else in the room was able to hear the sound of her newborn crying, Grace wasn't sure if her baby was breathing. Her sister figured out what was happening and lifted the mask off of Grace allowing her to hear the beautiful, clear cry of her very much alive baby.

The baby was still considered premature and needed to be whisked away to check that the heart and lungs were working properly. Grace had decided not to find out the gender during the pregnancy. It was too much for Grace to get attached to one more element of someone that might not come to be. They figured it would be an added surprise if everything worked out. Myles realized as the baby was back on its way to them that they hadn't looked yet to see if it was a boy or a girl. The baby was placed into Grace's arms and she looked under the blanket and announced it was a girl. Everyone cheered and cried simultaneously as if everyone had taken their first breath in a very long time.

Grace and Myles marveled at their miracle and were so excited to finally be at this anticipated moment. There was much celebrating between them both as they held their sweet girl in their arms. They were finally a family. They decided on the name Jordan for their daughter. It was a family surname of Grace's family. Jordan was born over seven pounds even though she was a few weeks premature so she didn't need any extra medical attention and they were all able to return home and out of the hospital together. Grace hadn't stood up for more than a few minutes at a time in weeks so her legs were quite weak. She was grateful to have her family there to lean on while she gained strength.

There was nothing in their apartment to welcome a baby. Grace and Miles couldn't bring themselves to purchase anything until they had a baby at home. Grace's dad and sister went out to buy everything from diapers to a nursing pillow, wipes, and a bassinet all in one fell swoop. They had not gotten a chance as a couple to take any birthing classes because of being on bed rest, so Myles especially didn't know exactly what to do. They were a little shaky at first but like taking the training wheels off of a bicycle, they got the hang of parenting their newborn.

As the months passed they relaxed into parenthood and started to make new friends that also had children the same age. By the time Jordan was old enough to toddle around, she also made some new friends of her own. As they all got the hang of family life, Grace mentioned the idea of having another baby to Myles. She knew she always wanted more than one child. Her relationship with her sister was unique, important, and meaningful to her. She wanted Jordan to have the same opportunity to share her life with a sibling of her own. Myles could see the benefit of a sibling but was hesitant to go down the path they had gone down again to get Jordan here. Grace did some research and asked her doctor questions about having another baby. She learned that every precaution that was taken during her pregnancy with Jordan would have to be taken again. She would have to move into the hospital and away from Jordan for a great deal of time. Grace didn't want to go through that again either.

When Grace and Myles were struggling with fertility early on they had discussed adopting. They even went to a seminar on international adoption before they tried IVF. They had learned a lot and decided to revisit the idea. For Grace, it wasn't important enough to have another pregnancy as much as it was to have another baby. When Jordan was two and a half they started the adoption process. They looked into Korea, but it was too expensive. They looked into China, but the process could take years. They had decided to pursue Guatamalla but then adoptions from there were shut down. Grace had traveled to Africa in her twenties and loved it, so they decided to look into adopting from Ethiopia. The adoption process from there was much more straightforward so they began their paperwork.

There were many fits and starts during their efforts to bring home another baby. It took over a year for all of the paperwork to be squared away and during that time the Ethiopian government had tried to shut down adoptions. They had been matched with a baby boy when he was five months old. His name was Addis and all they had were a few photos of him and a whole lot of hope. When Addis was eight months old Grace, Myles and Jordan got on a plane together and flew to Ethiopia to meet Addis. Jordan was three by then and was a trooper through the long journey. They stayed in a little room close to the orphanage and were a woozy mix of exhausted and excited by the time they got settled in. When the three of them got to the orphanage they were surprised to see that there were close to ten babies under the care of one caretaker. The babies were all quiet. Not because they weren't sad, hungry, or in need, but because they had already learned that no one come if they did cry. When they finally saw Addis they knew he was their boy. He smiled up at Jordan and they reached out for each other right away.

During their adoption visit the agency they had been using had got caught up in some red tape. They knew it was a possibility that they wouldn't be able to take Addis home on that trip but it was becoming clearer with each day there that not only wouldn't they be taking him home right away, but they wouldn't know just how much longer they would have to wait. They had to bring paperwork to a judge while in Ethiopia to be able to move the adoption any further along. When they got to the judge other American families were waiting with paperwork as well. Grace noticed the judge wasn't signing everyone's forms but had no idea why. When it was their turn to go up to her, she looked them over, looked at the papers, took her pen to the pages, and signed. Their paperwork was approved and they could continue adopting Addis, they just needed to go back home to New York and wait to be notified that he was ready to be picked up. Grace was part of an online community of people who had also adopted from Ethiopia, or were in the process like she was, and some of those people had been waiting for over a year. The familiar feeling of unwanted uncertainty set into Grace's stomach. Once again, she had gone so far down a path, that she had gotten her hopes up, and maybe like before she could be disappointed. Myles was supportive and encouraged them both to focus on Jordan, who was after all a fantastic distraction.

When Addis was one year old Grace and Myles got a call letting them know that they could return to Ethiopia to pick him up. Grace's mother came and stayed with Jordan while she and Myles flew back to Ethiopia to pick up their little boy. Once again Grace did not let herself get attached to the idea of any of this happening, but when they got to the orphanage, Addis was placed in their arms. This time they had a lot more ready to bring home a baby and had a baby bag packed for the flight home. It wasn't until Grace was sitting in her seat on the plane with Addis snuggled on her lap, that she fully allowed herself to believe this was happening.

Grace and Myles were the parents of a daughter and son, and they couldn't wait to reunite with Jordan when they got home.

Jordan was excited to see them home, and that was the official start of their family. Jordan got to hold Addis on her lap even though she could barely get her head over his to see out. She began talking to him telling him what everything around them in the room was. She pointed out who their parents were, where he would be staying, and how they would play together. She told him he was her brother now, and that she would take care of him. Grace and Myles smiled as they watched and no matter what roundabout ways they had to go through to get to this moment, each turn had paved the way for this family, their family.

Chapter Ten

Shannon

E veryone from the South seems to have a bit more color in their wardrobe, a more musical tone to their twang, and a flair for decorations. Shannon loved bright, festive holidays and had turned her passion for decorating into a career. She owned an event-planning business that she built from the ground up. She was a hard worker, and she took her work seriously—but she had a silly side that she revealed daily. Anyone who worked with her knew, at some point in the day, you were bound to hear her high-pitched and contagious laugh.

Shannon grew up in the suburbs of Alabama but moved to Birmingham to study art in college. She planted her roots there and found a network of friends who, like her, hardly left Birmingham after college. Shannon was able to partic-ipate in an art fellowship in Philadelphia for a few summers and had a blast. She enjoyed navigating a new city, meeting new people, and having the opportunity to grow her art with so many inspiring mentors. One mentor in particular caught her eye. After taking his class on Pop Art and watching him teach with so much personality, Shannon was smitten.

"Alistair Clough is my future husband—he just doesn't know it yet," Shannon joked to a classmate one afternoon.

"You might want to keep that information from his wife," her classmate said. Shannon was disappointed to learn that news and ended the story she had drafted in her head about their future together. When she came back to Philly the next summer, she ended up in another of Alistair's lectures and remembered why she was so taken with him. She imagined his wife, and how happy she must be to laugh, have in-depth conversations, and live surrounded by great art all the time.

When the second summer ended, Shannon returned to Birmingham. She painted, gave children's art lessons, and dedicated the rest of her time to building her business. By the time she learned that Alistair was going to be doing a residency in Alabama from a few friends from Philadelphia, they had already reached out to him to see if there were any openings for them. Shannon wanted to join. She wasn't his only fan- everyone loved working with him. If they could get the opportunity, they all agreed to go together.

A few months went by before she heard from a friend that he'd received a spot—then another friend heard they were in, too. Shannon had started to give up on the idea when her letter came a few days later. When Shannon listened to Alistair talk on the residency's first day, she tried not to let her thoughts wander as to whether or not he and his wife had had their first baby yet. She tried to snap herself back into focus, but she knew by now he must have recognized her. He smiled at her so warmly that her composure melted.

Shannon made sure to keep reminding herself why she was attending Alistair's residency: she loved his lectures, and she learned something new whenever she participated in workshops. She was there because it was a great opportunity to work on her art with her close friends. She kept revisiting these reasons whenever she realized she was spending too much time putting together her outfits, or wasting time trying to come up with questions to ask during Alistair's lecture just to have a chance to speak with him. She had no interest in becoming involved with a married man.

Shannon kept her imagination in check by spending time with her friends and maximizing her time in the workshops. During the last week, one of her friends invited her out with a bunch of other artists, including Alistair. Shannon was reluctant to go because she didn't see the point—she was sure Alistair Clough had no idea who she was, and it would be really awkward if he started talking to her. Shannon knew so much about him and yet, she thought, he knew nothing about her.

One of her friends convinced her to go, promising that she would have fun and that if she didn't, he would walk her home. Shannon agreed—and was glad she did. While she was sitting around a table with the group of artists, she overheard that Alistair's divorce was final. She didn't know everything about Alistair Clough after all. He wasn't about to become a father with the wife of his dreams—he was about to be divorced.

Shannon didn't restart her daydreaming about Alistair, though. She talked to him that night and was pleasantly surprised that he actually *did* know who she was. She went home content, having enjoyed her pleasant conversation with him. Her friend who invited her out saw the two of them speaking; the next day, he mentioned to Alistair that Shannon had a bit of a crush on him. Shannon wasn't aware of this, though, and when the fellowship was over, everyone went back to their lives. She had a very busy holiday season with her company, planning, coordinating, and successfully executing several holiday parties. The month of January was still busy with New Year's parties, company events, and planning for a few Superbowl parties. She was working more than she ever had.

When February rolled around, she welcomed the quiet. When her phone rang one evening with an unrecognizable number, she let it go to her voicemail.

"Hi Shannon, this is Alistair Clough," the voice on the message said. "I talked with you a few months back in Alabama, where I believe you live. Anyway, I am coming to Birmingham for a few days and wondered if you would like to meet for drinks."

The message ended, and Shannon couldn't move. She kept staring at the same splinter of wood on the floor. She wondered, giddy yet cautious if she'd really heard that message correctly. She listened again as her heart beat a bit faster in her chest. Alistair Clough just called her, left a message on her voicemail, and asked her out for a drink. The fictitious story she'd made up years before was possibly coming to life. She grabbed onto her enthusiasm and decided she would not call him back until the next day. She didn't want to seem too excited—even though that is exactly what she was.

Shannon met Alistair for drinks the next week; although she had been obsessed about what she would say, or what topics they would talk about, or how he would perceive her, once she was sitting across from him she didn't have to think about anything at all. The conversation and laughter flowed easily. Shannon sensed a certain level of comfort already developed between them—they shared their mutual love of art and had a lot of common friends. And, of course, they had already spent the last few years working together, even though they hadn't spoken to each other before tonight.

Alistair asked her question after question about her childhood, her business, and her dreams for the future. She asked him about his upbringing and what it was like to live in America after growing up in Scotland—and she even braved asking about his first marriage. He confessed that his ex-wife was never okay with the traveling he had to do. He said that she had a good heart, but he described her as a "half glass empty" kind of person. They had thought about starting a family, he shared, but his gut told him it was time to end things before they went as far as having a child together. He admitted to wanting to get married again—next time, to the right person.

Shannon listened and watched Alistair as he spoke. In her mind, little check marks ticked boxes whenever he said something that made her like him even more. By the end of the evening, she only had one imaginary check placed on the "con" column. How would she get to know someone more if she didn't even know when she would see him again? She hadn't thought about those details before she went out for drinks. She didn't expect to be as enthralled with him as she was. She had wondered if she had built him up in her mind, but when she finally sat across from him, drinks in hand, she was pleasantly surprised to find that he was even more engaging than he she had hoped. They agreed to stay in touch until they figured out when they could meet again.

Alistair called her the next day, and they talked for hours. After that, not a day passed without them talking on the phone.

Eventually, they met in person, again and again and again, until they both realized they wanted to live together in the same city. Shannon decided she would try living in Philadelphia and travel back for events in Birmingham. She could still work from home planning her events and then return to Birmingham for the events themselves.

Shannon let her art students know she was moving, and once she'd settled in, she figured that she could try teaching in Philly. She had never lived with a boyfriend before and, although things were serious between her and Alistair, she had never spent more than a few days at a time with him. She hoped this move would be successful—but just in case, Shannon sublet her apartment. She was already taking a big leap into this new relationship; she wasn't about to give up her whole life for it.

Living together went better than she had expected: they faced a few housekeeping disagreements but became able to navigate conflicts easily. They both made each other laugh before any topic got too heavy. Soon, it became clear to Shannon and Alistair that their relationship wasn't temporary. Although Alistair wanted to get married again, he had cold feet about getting in front of everyone in his life again, as if to say, "Take two—thanks for coming out for the first one, but this time I mean it." Shannon knew that he was apprehensive, and even though she wanted to get married, she wanted to wait until he was as enthusiastic about the idea as she was.

Shannon was patient and could wait a while for a good thing—but she was in her early thirties, and they'd both agreed they wanted children, so she knew they couldn't wait forever. Shannon had enough to focus on between her company, all the travel, and her new life in Philadelphia, but her patience didn't stop her from planning her ideal wedding event. She knew Alistair wasn't ready, but she wanted a plan in place for when he was.

She kept herself busy getting to know her new city, so on a Sunday night after dinner when she looked up to find Alistair down on one knee, she didn't understand why he was on the ground. He handed her a note and when she read "Shannon, will you marry me?" She was so surprised. Alistair had managed to plan out a whole evening of dessert, scheduled phone calls with Shannon's family, and a beautiful ring that showcased her grandmother's diamond.

Not only had Alistair decided he was ready to move forward, but when she asked him when he thought they should marry, he was eager to do so as soon as possible. A dedicated planner, Shannon had thought about her wedding plans in detail and wanted at least a few months to solidify the ideas she had and run them by Alistair. "Why are you in such a hurry all of a sudden?" Shannon playfully asked him.

"I don't want to waste any more time," he said. "I want to have a family, and I have already lost so much time married to the wrong person—I don't want to lose out anytime with the right one."

Shannon wrapped her arms around Alistair and cried. Sometimes she couldn't believe she was actually about to marry Alistair Clough, the artist who she had such a big crush on for so many years. She loved the real boyfriend/fiancé Alistair even more than the version of him that she had made up in her head.

Their wedding was a colorful combination of the two of them, tasteful yet artistic. Shannon's creativity shone through, and she loved collaborating with Alistair for their big event. They combined his Scottish family Tartan into the decorating, as well as a mixture of her family's crystal on all of the tables. Instead of typical place cards for their guests in the weeks leading up to the big day, Shannon and Allister would come together nightly to paint stones for each of their guests to help guide them to the right table. These stones matched the small table decorations they painted for each table. They enjoyed mixing their creativity together for this big celebration of the two of them.

Once they were married, they agreed to start trying for a baby immediately. After six months without a pregnancy, Shannon's doctor referred them to a fertility specialist. Shannon was given medication and hormone shots to take at home. She was apprehensive but willing to give it a try for a month or two. On the medication, she felt horribly moody, bloated, and not at all like herself—she also didn't get pregnant. She stopped the treatments and started to feel better. Shannon suggested that they switch to a different doctor, and when they did, they learned that their fertility issues lay with Alistair and not her.

The new doctor suggested they try in-vitro fertilization to see if it might help them conceive. The first round didn't work though, and they were both disappointed. They had hoped to have a baby. Shannon was grateful they started trying right after they got married and that they got married when they did: she didn't realize how long this process could take or how much it could cost. At the visit to the doctor following their first unsuccessful attempt, both Alistair and Shannon became encouraged by the doctor and decided to try IVF again the following month.

Time didn't feel like it was on their side when they were waiting for news from the doctor: the two weeks from implantation to a pregnancy test seemed impossibly long. They went out to dinner and movies and took some long walks, trying to pass the downtime when they weren't busy with work. Even after an hour of work, they'd remember that they were waiting for news, no matter how hard they tried to distract themselves.

When they, at last, got a call letting them know that Shannon was indeed pregnant, she and Alistair both cried. The relief of knowing that they *could* get pregnant was something to celebrate. They held their secret tight to their chests; when Shannon miscarried at six weeks, their excitement turned to devastation.

Shannon took time to mourn the loss of her pregnancy and then got back into gear to try again. She and Alistair completed another transfer with the doctor and this time, when she found out she was pregnant, Shannon sat quietly with her hands on her belly and imagined surrounding her little growing baby with safety, love, and encouragement. She wasn't generally the most spiritual person, but she connected to her baby right then and there.

Shannon and Alistair were overjoyed—and although they didn't share their news with many people, they kept talking about it to one another with delight. They were going to be parents, and they spent those first few nights after hearing their news absorbing that idea. They daydreamed of what their child would do when they grew up. They joked that he or she might be a better artist than both of them and then what would they do? They came up with the absolute weirdest names that they could think of, never intending to use any of them. Side by side on their couch, they held hands and smiled, reveling in their new roles in life.

Shannon's pregnancy began uneventfully. She had no morning sickness, and—other than being a bit more tired and hungry—she felt like herself. She continued working and was thrilled when she was able to share the news with coworkers. Her first few ultrasounds were incredible to behold. Both Alistair and Shannon squeezed each other's hands as they watched their child's heart beating on the monitor.

Shannon enjoyed being pregnant and was grateful to no longer need the constant medical attention that came with the fertility treatments. She was able to continue her quiet, normal pregnancy until about the twentieth week. At a routine appointment, the doctor noticed that there were fluid-filled sacs around the embryonic sac. This seemed to alarm the doctor, as he admitted to not being familiar with such a thing. He referred Shannon to a specialized radiologist, and after waiting a grueling ten days, she finally had an appointment. Alistair accompanied her and this time while they squeezed each other's hands it was to hold on to each other in hopes of reassuring news. The specialist took quite a long time studying the monitor before saying anything. He clicked on different margins of what looked like the outside of her uterus, but Shannon just stared on silently.

As hard as it was to sit waiting as the specialist worked, measuring and studying the monitor, Shannon was grateful for how thoroughly he paid attention to details. After what seemed like close to an hour, he turned to them and explained some of what he saw. He explained that the fluid sacs were just fluid sacs and that they weren't of concern, but he noticed something unique about the umbilical cord. He called it a Velamentous cord, which happens when the cord spiderwebs out and attaches to many different veins. A Velamentous cord attaches to the placenta in an unusual way, and the baby will usually come a bit early as a result. The specialist explained that these appear in roughly one percent of pregnancies and that they would continue monitoring the pregnancy closely.

That night, Shannon and Alistair tried to process everything they heard in the office. Alistair thought he remembered the specialist mentioning something about "bleeding on the brain," and Shannon thought she heard something about a possible chance of hemorrhaging. They wished doctors handed out a flier. They weren't sure what they needed to do next, so they made a list of what to ask at the next appointment and conducted their own research online.

"Hey, you are finally part of the one percent," Alistair joked.

"Yes, it looks like I am. Fancy that!" said Shannon. She didn't want to be in that club; she wanted to go back into the club for women with uneventful pregnancies.

The month following that appointment went normally: the baby was growing on track and the cord or sacs didn't cause any issues. When Shannon and Alistair asked about possible bleeding on the baby's brain, their regular doctor said that sometimes, with an obstruction and lack of space, bleeding could happen—but it wasn't happening to their baby. Shannon also asked about hemorrhaging, and the doctor said that it would be very rare and that, in the very unlikely event it did happen, the hospital already would be the safest place to be.

Just a few weeks later, and six weeks earlier than expected, Shannon went into labor. Alistair was able to get to the hospital right away.

In most cases, women in their third trimester are tested for Group B strep before giving birth because it can be easily passed from the mother to the baby and cause dangerous complications for the newborn. Since Shannon went into labor so early, they didn't have time to test her. Instead as a precaution, they treated her (and all untested women) with penicillin in an IV drip, just as they would for someone who has Group B strep. Shannon was fine with this precaution—except that she had no idea that she was allergic to penicillin until it was already wreaking havoc on her system. She went into anaphylaxis, and her tongue and throat swelled. The team of nurses quickly responded by stopping the penicillin and flushing it out with an IV of Benadryl so that Shannon could breathe. Once that pretty important element was resolved, she was able to start pushing.

The many issues that Shannon and Alistair feared thankfully never came to pass: there were no brain issues and no hemorrhaging. The only unusual element of surprise was the unique umbilical cord that tethered Shannon to her baby. Nurses who weren't even part of her birth came in to admire their Velamentous cord because it was so rare. Shannon studied the cord herself and smiled: it looked to her like a rope with multiple strands that connected her to the baby. As an artist, she looked at the colors and the shapes and saw the beauty of its uniqueness. Just like the cord she and this baby had a distinctive, strong bond—since they had already gone through so much together.

After a few weeks in the NICU, Alistair and Shannon brought home their healthy baby boy, whom they named Solomon. They were thrilled to be home as a family for the first time. Adjusting to parenthood is challenging for everyone, and Shannon and Alistair were no exception—but diaper blowouts, sleepless nights, and round-the-clock feedings paled in comparison to the concerns that they had to deal with getting their son into the world. They got the hang of parenting and admitted to each other that they thought they were quite good at it.

Eventually, and with the help of childcare and friends, both Shannon and Alistair were able to return to work. Shannon was able to work from home a few days a week so that she could be near her son. Alistair's work required him to travel; while this used to be something he loved, he didn't like being away from his family for very long. When he was in town, he did his best to make it home for a family dinner most nights. When he was away, he would FaceTime daily, so he didn't miss any milestones.

Alistair and Shannon wanted more than one child, but they hadn't planned when they would start trying again—and, it turned out, they didn't have to. Without any fertility assistance, they got pregnant on their own a year after Shannon had their son. Shannon was unaware that she was pregnant since her cycle hadn't started again. She happened to have some pregnancy tests in her bathroom drawer and took one when she noticed familiar feelings. When it was positive, she made an appointment to see her doctor.

At the appointment, the doctor informed her that she was about twelve weeks along, but her hormone levels were very low. Shannon was told to come back to re-check a few days later—and eventually, she miscarried. The bleeding went on for days, and she ended up in the hospital.

The miscarriage made Shannon realize how much she wanted to have another baby, so once enough time had passed and she had the go-ahead from her doctor, she and Alistair tried again. Shannon got pregnant again, but she kept her excitement in check, placing her energy into her son, family time, and work. When she reached her twelve-week ultrasound and the baby was growing normally, Shannon felt a calmness she hadn't experienced since before beginning the pregnancy. She tried to take each moment as it came, knowing that nothing in making children had been predictable for her so far.

Shannon's two pregnancies had nothing in common—except for the fact that both were flooded with rare, difficult conditions. In her second pregnancy, she was nauseous for the entire pregnancy; she was sick, tired, and drained most of the time. In her third trimester, Shannon was granted a short window of time where she regained her energy and started to feel herself again. Her belly grew, and she was able to care for her son as well as work a few hours a day.

One night in her last trimester, after putting her son to bed, Shannon walked back to her bedroom to read. As she opened up her book, she had trouble concentrating—she kept rubbing the souls of her feet together because they were so itchy. She couldn't seem to relieve the itching, so she stood up and dragged her soles along the hardwood floor for relief.

She called her doctor's office that night, and they told her to come in right away for a blood test to see if her liver was working properly. When the results came back showing that Shannon's numbers were off, the doctor ordered more tests to find out what the level of bile salts was in her blood. The results confirmed that Shannon's discomfort was caused by something called cholestasis of pregnancy: a liver condition that occurs when bile, produced by the liver, doesn't get stored normally by the gallbladder because pregnancy hormones change how a gallbladder functions. As a result, bile spills out of the liver and into the bloodstream—and the spillage causes intense itching. Shannon was given some medication to try, but it didn't really help. Due to the increased risks of waiting, at thirty-seven weeks, the doctor suggested that Shannon be induced. The itching was so bad leading up to the induction that Shannon scratched her skin raw. She took medication in an effort to quell the itching and it worked, but not well enough.

Shannon had her close friend Ann on call to accompany her to the hospital. Shannon was so grateful to the caregiver she had hired for her son because Alistair was in Europe, working. As hard as it was to not have him by her side, this was something they knew might happen. His travel came with the job and sometimes, he'd have to miss things—like his wife having a baby. He stayed in contact and had the caregiver's info as well as Shannon's friend's number. This way, when Shannon couldn't talk, he would still be briefed on the birth process.

By the time the induction date arrived, Shannon couldn't stand the itching anymore—she thought she might go crazy. It was distracting her from being able to focus on the fact that she was about to have another baby. Once she was checked in and admitted to a room, Shannon fell asleep for a bit; she had been so exhausted from all the scratching. She wasn't sure how long she was asleep, but she woke up to nurses bustling around her.

"We are going to give you an IV of Pitocin to help start your labor, as well as an IV for fluids," said a nurse who Shannon didn't recognize as she took her arm to prepare the IV. This was all moving faster than Shannon had expected. Her friend had gone to get something to eat and hadn't gotten back yet. Alistair was across the ocean. Suddenly, Shannon felt so alone—and yet the IV was starting.

"The anesthesiologist is on his way as well to give you your epidural," said the same nurse. Shannon felt like she had no chance to ask questions or slow down to process what was happening. She wasn't quite as alert as she thought she should be— like she was asked to run a marathon without any training, water, or even shoes. There was no time to protest, though, because the race had already begun: the anesthesiologist was in the doorway and on his way to her bed. He was friendly enough, but he didn't waste much time. She wondered if this pace was by design. Perhaps, if pregnant women were given the freedom to say when they were ready for an epidural, they might take hours. Shannon surrendered herself to what was happening. She was too exhausted to do anything else.

Shannon listened to the anesthesiologist's instructions as he gave them. She turned onto her right side and arched her back. As much as she disliked the idea of a needle going into her spine, she followed his direction and tried not to tense up. He told her when he was inserting the needle, and once he was done, he let her know that the needle seemed to have punctured the membrane covering her spinal cord. He explained that it happened accidentally, especially when the patient is petite and muscular like Shannon, and that it could cause a bad headache a few hours after giving birth due to a tremendous build-up in pressure from the spinal fluid leaking.

"This happens to about one percent of women," the anesthesiologist explained.

Shannon tried to listen to what he was telling her, but she was in shock. It didn't seem possible that so many "rare" things that happened to some women during pregnancy had all happened to her. She hoped that someone else was taking notes at this point because her contractions were coming—she needed to focus on having a baby. Ann returned just in time for her to push.

"I'm so sorry—I grabbed a sandwich at the worst possible time," Ann said. "Tell me what you need. I am here now."

"I need this baby to come out, and for you to hold my hands," Shannon said.

Grumpy from the epidural news, Shannon was relieved to have a familiar face looking back at her. She put her forehead on the top of Ann's hands and closed her eyes. She didn't know how she was going to deliver this baby, care for the one she had at home, be responsible for two humans, and make it through any of her future if she was this exhausted right out of the gate. She had never had a panic attack before—and this certainly wasn't a very convenient time for her first one—but her chest tightened, and she started breathing quickly. Ann figured out what was happening and bent down to meet Shannon's eyes.

"This is really hard, and not the most ideal circumstances, but I am here, and you can do this," Ann instructed Shannon to keep her eyes open and to list off the items that she saw in the room around her. At first, Shannon couldn't keep her eyes open and wasn't sure she wanted to play along, but Ann wasn't going to leave her alone—so she recited what she saw.

"I see you, yellow curtains, a shiny linoleum floor, white bed sheets, expensive equipment, and a bunch of people in scrubs, including but not limited to the guy who fucked up my epidural," Shannon whispered into Ann's ear. Ann laughed, even though it wasn't meant to be funny. Shannon's breathing slowed down and Ann reminded her to take one breath at a time.

Shannon moved her head to the center of the bed and slid her numb half upright as best as she could. "I think I need to push," she called out to everyone and no one in particular.

With Ann by her side and the doctor preparing the tools for delivery, Shannon was relieved that the doctor checked and agreed it was go-time. She couldn't wait any longer, and when instructed, she took a deep breath, bore down, and pushed. When the baby came out, there was silence, not the loud cry everyone expected—but the doctor reassured Shannon that her new baby boy was breathing. The doctor and nurses examined him, and as quickly as they could, they put him on Shannon's chest.

Shannon and Ann stared at the baby, taking him in. His face was pretty mushed from the birth, and he looked a little loopy, but Shannon could tell he was going to be beautiful. Ann hardly left their side while Shannon and the baby were still in the hospital. When they were released, Ann took Shannon home, and they introduced the baby to his big brother, who looked at his tiny little hands.

"Can I touch him?" he asked. Ann helped him clean his hands and he sat up on the couch next to Shannon. He curled his baby brother's little fingers into his hands.

"You are his big brother," Shannon said.

"I am, cuz I am so much bigger," he said as he compared the sizes of their hands.

Shannon was relieved to be home and grateful that Ann and the caretaker were there with her. She nursed the baby, and when he fell asleep, she put him in the bassinet beside her to take a rest. She fell asleep, and when she woke up, she had no idea how long she had been sleeping. She tried to sit up—but her head felt so heavy and hurt something awful. She closed her eyes, unable to look at anything when she was in so much pain. She did her best to muster sound to come out of her to call for Ann. This was no ordinary headache: this felt like a bowling ball had just been thrown at her head.

Shannon remembered the anesthesiologist telling her to look out for headaches, but he should have warned her that the pain could be excruciating. Every time she tried to lift her head, it was as if a ton of bricks were being piled on top of her, trying to keep her head down. She told Ann she needed to get back to the hospital quickly. By the time she got into the car, her vision was blurred. She had to lie down in the back seat.

When Shannon got to the hospital, the medical staff told her that she was in seizure range. Ann was able to explain what had happened and why Shannon was in so much pain. When she was seen by a doctor, he explained that the pain was from her brain sagging and rising. If she had waited any longer to get help, this could cause detachment and hemorrhaging. The leaking spinal fluid caused low pressure in the spinal column, which caused the brain to sag whenever she sat up or stood. The doctor told her that they needed to stop the leaking using something called a blood patch, and an anesthesiologist would give her another epidural and transfer her own blood into her spinal cord to clot the leak.

Shannon was exhausted and had reached far past her point of pain tolerance; she needed relief as quickly as possible. She vowed, at that moment, to be done with her baby-making business once she had recovered.

The blood patch worked, and Shannon began to feel so much better. Her body was exhausted and in need of a week-long nap. When she got home, it was hard for her to imagine caring for her two small children. Fortunately, Alistair was coming home a few days later, and Ann insisted on staying with her until he returned.

Shannon had endured more hiccups during her pregnancies than anyone else she had ever heard of. If there was a bizarre, random side effect that could happen while pregnant, Shannon had it. At home recovering, Shannon reminded herself that she was on the other side of her struggles now—and she had two healthy, beautiful sons to show for it. She knew it would take some time to adjust after the intensity of what she went through. There was trauma having gone from itching to induction, failed epidural to insane headaches, and—somewhere in there—pushing out a baby.

Two days later, Shannon went online to share the news of the birth with her college friends. She wrote a quick paragraph about the wackiness she went through, posted a photo, and pressed send. As she sat in front of the screen, she started to Google: first, she searched for any long-term side effects that could occur in a baby whose mother has taken anti-itch medication. Next, she looked up what could happen to a baby born to a distressed mother. From there, the search spiral continued; she looked up "bonding with your baby" and read that a mother should spend the first forty days by the baby's side. Shannon decided she'd already screwed up because she'd needed to go back to the hospital and spent time away from the baby. She panicked, suddenly feeling like she wasn't capable of handling the role of raising one child, let alone two.

As Shannon searched for more and more worst-case scenarios online, she got an email from one of her friends from school. She had seen the email from Shannon and reached out to say congratulations. She also asked how Shannon was doing—given what Shannon had gone through, her friend was concerned. Shannon immediately wrote back and was honest about not feeling herself. Her friend called Shannon and suggested that she seek help for postpartum depression. She told her to not wait—it would only get worse. Shannon couldn't handle anything else getting worse; she talked to her doctor, got diagnosed, and got help right away.

Shannon's situation had been an endless flow of challenges, and she knew that, without her support system around her, she wouldn't have healed as well as she did. She saw, from her experience, a gaping flaw in maternal care for postpartum women. There is a check-up right away for the baby, but most women have to wait six weeks to be seen by their OB after giving birth—and at that appointment, the focus is mostly on the physical healing from having a baby.

Shannon had to do extensive research to find support groups for new moms—and most of the groups she found were only accessible to women who could afford to pay a small fortune to join. There was almost nothing available free of charge to support new moms. Shannon decided this needed to change and reached out to the one organization she'd found that offered free services. It was a Jewish women's group, and Shannon's first question was "Do I have to be Jewish to be involved?"

The woman on the other end of the line explained to Shannon that the service is for anyone who wants to use it—or anyone who wants to volunteer for it—so Shannon asked what was involved in becoming a volunteer. The program was definitely a time commitment, but Shannon wanted to be there to help a new mom when needed. When her youngest baby was about a year old, she completed her training. These days, when a call comes in requesting help for a new mom, Shannon makes herself available to step up. She is proud to be part of a visiting care program for new moms and grateful that she can help someone when they need it most.

Chapter Eleven

Brie

As a little girl, Brie learned the order in which she was expected to do things. Even the stories her mother told her at night all involved princesses finding their prince. Once the princess found her prince, they planned the wedding. Story after story, movie after movie, dress-up game after dress-up game all ended the same way: a wedding! Brie understood that she wasn't a princess, but she knew she was supposed to find herself a prince, nonetheless.

In high school, when her friends started dating, Brie set her focus on getting into a good college. When she was in college, she went to parties, occasionally had a few too many drinks, made out with a few college friends, and even had a few one-night stands—but she never met anyone she wanted to be in a relationship with. She had a clear plan for her studies; she was happy to keep her eye on the prize of finishing college at the head of her class. Once she graduated, she moved back home briefly to Hinsdale, Illinois, a quiet suburb outside of Chicago. Her plan was to work in finance for a bit before figuring out her next steps.

Brie's first job out of college was as a financial-services assistant, which basically meant that she sold insurance. She hated it—but the numbers came easily to her, the paperwork was boring but straightforward, and her co-workers were fine. She just didn't find any creativity in the job. She worried that if she didn't make a change, she would be stuck living at home, selling insurance for the rest of her life.

Brie's parents were happy to have her home. She contributed a bit of money as well as did her part to cook and clean the house. Her younger brother, who was going to community college and also living at home, was grateful to have his sister back. Brie enjoyed everyone's company—but her mother was always asking Brie questions she didn't know how to answer.

"Have you met any nice boys at work?" her mother asked.

First off, Brie wasn't a girl anymore—so when her mother asked about "boys," it made Brie realize that her mother still didn't notice that she was an adult. Secondly, her mother asked her this practically every other day. Did she think in the small office of ten employees that a new "boy" would just walk in one day and sweep her off her feet?

"Not today, Mom—I mostly work with the same few people every day, and not too many of them are viable options," Brie would answer politely.

Her mother kept asking—and although the question didn't bother her in the beginning, Brie noticed that her mother wasn't the only one curious about her personal life. Her friends, her cousins, and even her co-workers hinted about available guys that Brie might want to meet. Brie tried to ignore their questions and curiosity about her love life, but after a while, it started to frustrate her. She went on a few dates to appease everyone. She met some really interesting people that she wanted to become friends with, but she didn't find anyone with whom she had real chemistry.

One of her close guy friends, Todd, had started out as a dating thing. They went out a few times, had a ton in common, and liked each other's company. When Brie was in a sexual mood, they would have sex. Occasionally, she would sleep over at his place, watch a movie, and have coffee the next day—but she never wanted to stay any longer than that. She cared for Todd and valued him as a friend—and sometimes, a friend with benefits—but she never wanted to have **a conversation** about their status. She avoided bringing up anything that had to do with dating, boyfriends or girlfriends, or commitment. She avoided all of those words because she wasn't interested.

"You cool with us, like this?" Todd would ask occasionally.

"Yup, you?" Brie would respond quickly, wanting to change the subject.

For the most part, this arrangement worked well for Todd, but sometimes he would want more from Brie than she wanted to give.

Brie wanted more from her job than it could offer her, so she decided to go back to school. She applied to MBA programs that offered international study tours. She aimed high and applied to Columbia, Stanford, USC, and Booth in Chicago. She assumed she would not get into her top choice, which was Columbia, and would end up staying in Chicago, but she got into every school she applied to. Columbia even offered her such a great financial aid package that it would have been more expensive for her to stay in Chicago for school. She had never lived in New York—she had never even visited. She was nervous, but also ready to see more than the middle of the country.

New York was every bit as busy, hectic, colorful, and alive as Brie had imagined it would be. Within the first week of the program, she knew she made the right decision to study there. She met like-minded, focused people who had similar goals to hers and knew that some of them would be her friends for life. They took school business trips around the world to different cities, and Brie felt like she learned more during her time in this program than she had learned in all her years of school prior.

Not once did anyone in her program ask her on a date, what her relationship status was, or if she was straight, bi, or gay. No one was focused on anything other than getting as much out of the MBA program as it had to offer. They'd all graduate in under two years and then everyone would scatter back to their homes—but while at Columbia, the subject of conversation was all business.

As the program reached its final term, Brie needed to decide where she would go next. New York was fun, but she didn't want to stay. She loved her family and missed being close to them—however, she knew that she didn't want to move back into their house. She decided to look for jobs in Chicago. That way she would live close enough to them, but also have her own place in the city. She applied to many jobs online, from the VP of business development at a cereal company to numerous low-paying startup positions to being an advisor for a program at Northwestern. She ended up with a VP position at an established food company, where she was hired to help rebrand and promote healthier versions of their existing products.

Brie signed a lease on a small apartment in Lincoln Park, a beautiful neighborhood on the north side of Chicago. There was a lot of greenery, a huge park, and many gardens around the neighborhood. Brie's office was in downtown Chicago, so choosing Lincoln Park made sense: there were a lot of younger apartment-dwellers in the area, and her commute from her apartment to her office was under a half hour. In contrast to the job she took straight out of college, her new position was thrilling. She thought of it more as a career rather than a job, and her dedication became quickly apparent to her team at work.

Her weekdays were filled with work meetings, lunches, dinners, and events. She made new friends through work and also had a good group of friends from college who had also made their way to live in Chicago. On the weekends, she would meet them for drinks and dinner. Sometimes Todd would make the hour-long drive to join her for the weekend. They would go see a band that they both loved or watch a new movie that they had both waited to see together. One night, Brie brought Todd with her to a friend's wedding. Brie's friends had started to get married, but this was Brie's first wedding invitation addressed to her "and a guest." Instead of going alone, she thought it would be fun to have Todd with her.

At the wedding, she and Todd danced, laughed, and drank together. When Todd went to the bathroom, her two friends honed in on her immediately.

"What is going on with you two? Are you together?" they asked. "You make a really cute couple."

"We're just really good friends," said Brie.

"Yes—and that is a tale as old as time," her friend pushed. "Two great friends can make a great couple."

That night, she and Todd had sex—not unusual for them, especially after a night of drinking. Brie had fun with Todd, and their sex was exciting. They knew each other's bodies well and knew what worked. Afterwards, while lying down next to each other laughing about all the different characters they had seen at the wedding, Todd leaned over and looked into Brie's eyes. She looked back at him, trying to figure out why he got so serious, and then burst out laughing. Todd leaned in and kissed her.

"Brie, I love you," said Todd

This threw Brie. The kiss, his words—this is not what she expected from Todd. She thought they were both on the same page with their arrangement. She was uncomfortable with his honesty and didn't know quite how to respond.

"I love you too, Todd, but I...um, I'm not sure...when you said what you just said..."

"You don't have to say anything, Brie. If you don't feel the same way, I would rather you didn't say anything at all." Todd said as he packed up his bag to go.

Brie didn't have any words that seemed to fit what Todd wanted to hear. She did love him, and she valued him in her life—she just wasn't in love with him. Brie didn't want to risk saying the wrong thing and hurting Todd more, so she let him leave.

Months went by, and Brie and Todd didn't have any contact at all. Brie went out with friends socially and enjoyed traveling for both work and relaxation. Occasionally, when there was time and the right opportunity presented itself, she would hook up with someone she met along the way. She had fun but still had no burning desire to take on a relationship with anyone.

As time passed and her thirtieth birthday approached, Brie started to take inventory. When friends or family asked her if she was involved with anyone, it always bothered her. She felt it was her business, her life, and her choice to live it as she saw fit. She didn't know if she would ever want to be in a relationship but for now, she had no interest. After doing some research, Brie learned that there was a name for how she felt: aromantic. An aromantic isn't interested in getting involved in a romantic relationship with anyone. As Brie read the definition, it was if each word was written just for her.

At this time, Brie's friends—who, a few years before, had gotten married—were now beginning to have children. When she went to visit her close friend Heather, who recently had given birth to a baby girl, Heather asked Brie if she wanted to hold the baby. Heather had named her baby Ava, and Heather gently placed Ava in Brie's arms.

"Hi, Ava," Brie said as she stared at this tiny being in her arms. Before she was even aware of her wave of emotions shifting inside her, Brie's eyes brimmed with tears. She was so amazed at this little person who had just changed the importance of Heather's life so quickly. Brie had always wanted to have children; she was fascinated by their sense of wonder and had hoped that one day, she would have the opportunity to raise a child of her own. She had just kept pushing the thought of motherhood aside because she hadn't met anyone with whom she would want to parent. She never had a real boyfriend, so the idea of a husband wasn't a concept she could really visualize. Holding Ava sparked a new goal for Brie, and at that moment she promised herself that, no matter what happened in her life romantically (or not), she wanted to be a mother.

Brie's career was in a good place, but she had goals for work that she wanted to meet by a certain age. She made a plan for herself to reach her career goals in two to three years—she wanted to become a mother by the age of thirty-five, regardless of her relationship status. It was important to her to be in a stable place in her career, to make sure her finances were solid, and still be young enough to parent a child. She knew it would be challenging to raise a child on her own, but she saw that her options were either parenting solo or not being a parent at all—and she was up for the job.

There were many single-parents-by-choice resources out there, and Brie would go down rabbit holes researching them. At night, during the time she used to spend socializing with friends or watching videos on social media, she read stories, joined Facebook information groups, looked into the costs of fertility, and learned about adoption options. She thought about whether it was important to her to use a sperm donor and have her own biological baby or if she wanted to adopt a baby. Both options came with their fair share of costs, emotionally and financially. In the case of fertility, there was a physical factor to consider as well.

By the time Brie was thirty-two, she met the career goal that she had set two years earlier. She had a daily routine that worked for her: she woke up each morning early enough for some mindfulness time, where she let her mind run with her daily tasks, plans, and meetings before calmly clearing her slate and getting ready for work. She had taken a mindfulness and yoga workshop and discovered this daily ritual to be a little gift of calm she could give herself each day.

One morning, she was sitting in her upright position, visualizing her thoughts coming and going like leaves in a stream—and all she could think about was Todd.

She grew sad that a few years had gone by since he'd left her apartment, and they hadn't talked since. She tried to bring herself back to the stream; instead, distracted, she made herself a note to reach out to him on her way to work.

On her phone, Brie looked up Todd and saw the last text exchange they had was almost three years prior. She started typing him a message but kept pressing delete every time she started. She put her phone away and looked out the window of her train on her commute to work. She decided she would call later from home when she had more time. She went to a yoga class, came home to shower, ate dinner, and then picked up the phone and just dialed. She didn't have a plan for what she would say, but she missed him and wanted to reach out. She hadn't asked herself what she wanted out of the call, but she hoped that—somehow—they could get their friendship back on track.

After the second ring, Todd answered the phone.

"Hi Todd, it's Brie—it's been a while, and I just wanted to say hi and see how you were," Brie said.

"Brie, wow, it has been a while. I'm well, I'm really well," Todd said.

Within a few minutes of making small talk, Brie could hear a tiny cooing sound in the background from Todd's end of the phone.

"Is that a baby?" Brie asked.

"Yeah, yes, it is. That's my daughter. I haven't talked to you in so long, I haven't had the chance to tell you. I got married and we have a two-month-old baby girl. She is incredible," Todd said.

Brie was shocked. She hadn't even considered the possibility that Todd would be married, and it was a lot to process. When they were hanging out, he seemed content with their arrangement, so she'd assumed that, like her, he would always be happy being "friends with benefits" —but he was married. It sank in that she and Todd would never be sexually active again.

The news also meant that Brie needed to admit to herself one of the reasons she called: she had hoped that maybe, just maybe, he would have moved on from the weird conversation they had that night a few years back and could return to how things were. She had also hoped that, if they could reestablish their friendship, maybe he would have been interested in co-parenting with her.

"Wow, Todd, congratulations! That's really wonderful news," Brie said.

"Thank you, Brie. It's really been amazing. We are pretty thrilled." said Todd.

Brie was happy for Todd, but sad that they wouldn't one day be parents together. She wasn't going to say any of this to him though. She wished him well and as she hung up the phone she wondered what would be her next steps to having a cooing baby of her own.

Chapter Twelve

Ally

Giving birth was an incredible experience for Ally. She had taken a hypno-birthing class with her husband Jack and learned to follow her own body's cues for the birth process. When she felt like it was time to push, she told one of the nurses, but because she was so calm, the nurse didn't believe her. Jack supported Ally by breathing along in unison with her.

This was Ally and Jack's first baby, and Ally had taken every class she could in preparation for becoming a mother. She ate the healthiest foods, carefully avoiding anything listed as off-limits for pregnancy. She took folic acid, a prenatal vitamin—even though it was too large for nauseous women like her to have to swallow—and she drank lots of water to stay hydrated. She made sure to get plenty of exercise. From the moment she knew she was pregnant, she became her baby's mama, and she was smitten with the growth of her belly and every movement within it.

When Zsazsa was placed in Ally's arms, the small hospital room filled up with color. Ally had never seen anything more beautiful. She stared at her tiny little baby, taking in every detail of her face and every crease on her fingers; she stroked the fine little hairs on her head. Ally was terrified that Zsazsa, so small and fragile, would break in her arms, but then Ally reminded herself that Zsazsa couldn't be broken any more than she already was. Zsazsa was born in the thirty-fifth week of pregnancy after being induced because Ally and Jack learned that Zsazsa's heart had stopped beating.

A few days earlier, on a Sunday, Ally was walking with her friend Tricia when she confessed that she hadn't felt the baby move all day.

"The baby is probably just stuck because I can feel a little leg all curled up," Ally said, hoping her friend would reassure her that there was no need to worry.

"You haven't felt movement all day? You should go in and be checked—just to be sure," Tricia said.

That night Ally went home, trying to ignore Tricia's concern circling around in her head. The next morning, when Ally went to see her midwife, the baby's heartbeat was undetectable. The midwife didn't have the ability to give her an ultrasound, so she suggested that Ally see her doctor right away. Ally held out hope on the way to her OB's office that all of the worst-case scenario evidence was wrong. She longed to let out the breath that she had been holding when her doctor rolled the sonogram wand warmly over her belly as the doctor discovered her baby's loud, healthy heartbeat. Instead, Ally watched her doctor's face change for what seemed like forever before she finally spoke.

"I'm so sorry, but your baby..."

The doctor didn't need to finish the sentence because Ally, already crying, understood. She had gone alone to the appointment, having convinced herself that she was worrying for nothing. Now, she wished Jack was by her side. Her doctor sent her to the hospital right away to be induced. She called Jack and asked him to meet her there. Once he arrived, they were placed in a windowless room and told that she would deliver the baby that day. It was too much to process—Ally was already numb from the shock that her baby was not going to be born alive.

Ally was raised to be her own advocate. She has a straightforward attitude and an embodied confidence that has served her well. She wasn't afraid to ask the questions that most women wouldn't in this situation: first if she had to stay and deliver on that day, or if she could go home for the night. Ally was glad she asked because she and Jack were able to go home for the night to grieve. At home, they held her belly and talked to the baby. They cried for the life that the baby wouldn't get to live, letting the baby know that he or she was loved, and would always be loved. That night gave them the time to make some peace with the situation.

Ally was raised within the anthroposophy philosophy of spirituality, and everything she had learned about death seemed to prepare her for this moment in time: in particular, death and dying were not to be feared, but rather honored and respected. She was raised with at-home funerals that included three-day vigils for the person who died as a way to care for their soul. These vigils allowed people to mourn at home with their loved ones and to say goodbye in a peaceful setting. The first phone call Ally made when she and Jack got home was to her aunt, who had arranged home funerals in the past so that she could have one for her baby. Once that arrangement was in the works, they began to call family to let them know and to give them time to travel, so that they could mourn together.

The next day at the hospital, Ally and Jack were given a room at the end of a hall—this time, with a window. Ally was given a gown and was introduced to the nurses who would be helping her during delivery, as well as to the therapist who came in to talk to them. Ally asked if, after the baby was delivered, they could take the baby home with them. They learned that this is not a typical practice with a stillborn baby, but they could, if they wanted to.

Ally was surprised by the number of assumptions made on behalf of new mothers giving birth. If she hadn't asked for it, she wouldn't have gotten the time to hold her baby—instead, the baby would have been sent to the morgue or crematorium. She learned that some parents don't even know that they can have a funeral for their baby. Ally and Jack had the night at home to research their options, but it was so upsetting to them that other people in the same situation would not have the time or opportunity at the hospital to say goodbye to their children.

Earlier in her pregnancy, Ally and Jack had decided to let the gender of their baby be a surprise. After delivering her sleeping baby, Ally couldn't wait to find out who she had been carrying all these months. She looked at her fully-formed, perfect little baby and saw that she had given birth to a baby girl. She became a mother the moment she knew she was pregnant, but when her husband looked at their daughter for the first time, Ally could see him become a father before her eyes. She loved the way he was able to accept the sadness of their situation and yet still be so proud of what they had made. Seeing him embrace both intense feelings simultaneously gave Ally permission to accept every emotion that swept over her. She was grateful that Jack was connected to her during this experience. They were able to turn down the dial of time and space in order to hold their daughter together as the world around them blurred.

Ally learned to take great care as she held her baby girl. After a baby dies in utero, their skin becomes delicate and paper-like. Her first motherly instincts were spot-on when Ally was afraid of her baby's fragility. Living or not, Ally was protecting her daughter and that immediate impulse grounded her and gave her hope.

Jack and Ally had toyed around with different names—but for a girl, they couldn't stop thinking about Zsazsa. The meaning of the name is "God is my oath," and they loved the purity of the meaning and its colorful personality. Before the birth, they worried about giving their baby such a unique name, and as they took in their baby, they wondered: since she wouldn't get to grow into her name, should they save it for the chance that one day, they might get to use the name again? But they couldn't look at their baby without seeing her as Zsazsa.

Despite the sadness that flooded in whenever Ally realized that Zsazsa would never grow old enough to start kindergarten, make a single friend, or give or receive any hugs, Ally experienced what it was like to love her unconditionally. The joy that existed in that room, despite all the pain, was palpable. Jack and Ally gave Zsazsa the middle name Joy because the eye of their storm swirling with grief was euphoria.

The bond between mother and child was sealed for Ally. When she was asked if she wanted to do an autopsy on Zsazsa, she couldn't imagine giving her baby over to be taken apart. Complications with the placenta were ruled out. The cause of death could have been the umbilical cord wrapped around her neck—for one in ten stillborn babies, this is the case. Even after extensive testing, the cause of death for many stillborn babies still remains unknown. For roughly one in one hundred pregnancies, this is just something that happens.

During her pregnancy, Ally didn't fully process the reality she was going to actually have a baby until around her eighth month. When she finally allowed herself to decorate the baby's room, she carefully unwrapped sheets, a wall hanging, and a mobile from their packages. She washed everything carefully before putting the room together. She grew excited about the sweetness of the little bunny rabbit being lifted up by a balloon on the wall hanging she hung. She learned later that the day she put together the nursery, her baby's heart had already stopped. When Jack and Ally eventually took apart the nursery decorations, they found the original packages that described the theme of the line as "Up, up and away." Ally stared at the little bunny floating upward into the sky.

When Ally was strong enough to leave the hospital, she and Jack left the way they had always planned: as a family, with their baby in tow. They were given instructions on how to care for Zsazsa while she was at home: they needed to keep her cold so that she could stay preserved. They filled the bassinet that they had with plastic bags and ice and gently placed Zsazsa in it, lifting her up every few hours to change the ice and lowering her back down. This time with her allowed both Jack and Ally the privacy to process their loss without the pressure they experienced at the hospital. It also gave them the time to honor Zsazsa with a proper funeral at home, surrounded by the people they loved.

Ally knew that her loss was difficult for most people to talk about or acknowledge—but still, she wondered what it would have been like for one friend to ask her about how her birth went, or for someone to have said "congratulations" instead of just "I'm sorry." Ally's wishes changed like the tide; her mood felt difficult for even her to follow. After the funeral was over and Zsazsa was no longer in the house with her, a whole new phase of processing began. Ally found herself avoiding people with babies. She was not only mourning the loss of having Zsazsa at home with her as a baby, but also the child she could have become, and how she would have been as a teenager or an adult.

Having a stillborn baby is not rare, but it is unusual for people to talk about it openly. Ally didn't want to walk around pretending that she didn't give birth to a beautiful daughter. She didn't want people to avoid the subject: she wanted to be asked about Zsazsa's birth. She wanted to share her experiences and stop feeling alone, but other people weren't open to hearing from her. People were afraid to upset her—and while she understood that impulse, she knew no one could possibly be capable of causing her more grief than she already felt. She needed to cry, express herself, and feel less alienated.

Ally learned to accept that her pain might not ever leave her completely. Those first few days following her baby's birth, her breasts still poured milk for the infant who had been tethered to her month after month. One part of her body was ready to care for a baby that another part of her body had already stopped supporting. She wondered if she would ever be able to trust the signals her body gave her again. While Ally was able to stop herself from going back in time and wondering if she could have changed this outcome, her ability to move forward wavered. She was now part of a quiet club that no one wanted to be a member of. No parent should ever have to outlive their child, and Ally felt Zsazsa had been robbed of her chance to live. The possibility that Ally played some part in the robbery weighed heavily on her.

Over time, Ally and Jack began to understand that the only way their baby's memory would be honored and kept alive was if they kept acknowledging her. They hung a photo of her on their wall. They talked about her, even if no one asked, and talked to each other about her. They got rid of most of the things that were meant to be hers but kept a few special ones as proof that they did have this baby, she was loved, and she came home for a time, even if she couldn't stay.

Reading stories of other families who'd experienced the specific pain of what she was feeling—the grief from a stillbirth or a miscarriage—helped Ally the most. The ache she had when she looked at her now empty nursery, or the fear that gripped her when she thought of trying again for another baby, had also been felt by the women in her books. It was liberating to read that when Ally had lost a sense of self, someone before her had experienced that too.

Ally knew of one woman, a friend of her sister's, who had given birth to a stillborn baby. Other than that, no one in her social circle could relate to her. "You can always try again" was often said to her to try to make her feel better—she knew whoever said it had good intentions, but it stirred up so much sadness inside her. It felt dismissive of Zsazsa to just move on and try to make a stronger baby this time. Every day for almost a year, the cells in her body had been working to grow this life that would not come to be—but on every one of those days, Ally created more and more of an attachment to being a mother to this baby. The outcome felt like a betrayal of her body, her hope, and her identity.

Ally didn't see how she would ever emerge from the depth of her sadness, but slowly, she found normalcy again. She took some needed space from the friends that, in their efforts to be comforting, only made things more uncomfortable for them and for her; she found solace in getting to know people who didn't know what she had gone through.

While mourning Zsazsa, Aly, and Jack made a promise to each other. They had locked eyes one day while standing next to Zsazsa, who lay on ice in their home, and swore that neither one would let the other go into despair. They were both devastated, but to honor their baby, they grew closer through their grief. Ally researched different ways to find support, and Jack agreed to join her. They went to a grief group for parents who lost babies around the same time they lost Zsazsa. They went to a psychic healer. Ally heard about dolphin therapy and wanted to find a place where they could try it themselves, in an effort to heal.

On days when they were apart, Ally and Jack still connected and communicated their grief to each other. Ally was so grateful to have Jack by her side, mourning along with her. They didn't deal with the loss in all the same ways, but they allowed space for each other's healing.

"I want to go and get the baby so I can put her in the stroller for a walk," confided Ally. "We got that nice stroller, and I didn't get a chance to use it. I know I sound like a little girl wanting to take her doll for a walk, but I miss Zsazsa so much—and if I could just take her for a walk, I might feel a little better."

"If you want me to get the stroller out, I will," Jack said. "We can even run it around the block just to see how fast it goes." Ally knew they wouldn't really do it, but Jack's offer made her feel better. One day, she was laughing at something Jack said, and it felt so good—but her happiness was quickly confiscated by a sense of betrayal to Zsazsa. It took her quite some time to allow herself to feel joy and sadness simultaneously. Jack had always encouraged her to present her authentic self to him and promised to do the same for her. This freedom that they shared around each other was the safety belt that kept them from falling during the wild ride they were on. Ally was able to rebuild parts of her identity that existed before she became pregnant.

Ally found a place in Mexico that did dolphin therapy, and she and Jack figured out a way to try it. It had been three months since Zsazsa was born, and through all of Ally's reading, she learned how the trauma from loss changes the brain. Dolphin ultrasound emissions, she'd read, have considerable healing potential for the cell membranes in the brain. Additionally, Ally had always loved dolphins—and once the therapy began, she realized that being in the water with them bestowed a sense of peace that she hadn't felt since before she got pregnant. Ally felt her cheek muscles fatiguing while she was in the water; she hadn't smiled that much in so long.

When Ally and Jack decided they wanted to try again, they were both nervous, but they felt ready. Neither of them wanted to put much thought into planning out if and when the timing would work to conceive—they both tried to keep the topic as light as possible. They were in Mexico soaking up the time together when she got pregnant. When they went to see the dolphins the morning after conception, as Ally watched them from the edge, one of them came out and put its nose right on her belly. Jack and Ally would later regard that as the official seal of approval and blessing of Ally's pregnancy. A few weeks after returning from Mexico, Ally learned that she was pregnant.

Together, Ally and Jack chose to tell no one: this time, she wanted to be as relaxed as possible. Ally would be considered high-risk, which meant more regular checkups. She made an active choice to eat whatever she wanted, skip all the prenatal yoga classes, and focus as little on the pregnancy as possible. She had already done the job of being overly careful, abundantly educated, and bonding with her belly-type pregnancy. It didn't turn out the way she had hoped, so she wanted to go with blasé for her second time around.

This didn't mean, to Ally, abandoning caring about the health of her baby—but distracting herself a bit for nine months was preferable to the anxiety that was brewing beneath her surface. She thought of all the young women who got pregnant and went on with their lifestyles, eating and drinking junk. She thought of the women who didn't know they were pregnant and took no measures to stay healthy. She thought about the women who worked physical jobs through their whole pregnancies without taking time off to care for their exhausted bodies—and still, most of them had healthy babies. The thing that they had in common was that they didn't overthink Mother Nature, and so Ally strove to be like them.

Ally and Jack didn't celebrate every milestone of pregnancy the way they had the first time. With every kick, flutter, or turn, they cautiously enjoyed each movement together in secret. Ally found herself teetering between her two babies: learning how to see herself as a mother-to-be without diminishing the memory of Zsazsa. With their first pregnancy, she and Jack loved the surprise of waiting to find out the gender, to see who their baby was, and to enjoy parenthood—but then they were robbed of the surprise pleasures with Zsazsa. This time, they wanted as much information as they could get about their baby, to savor every possible moment of bonding. They both tried to take each moment at a time without focusing on how the birth would go. When they found out they were having a boy, they thought about Zsazsa having a brother before they thought of themselves having a son.

Ally was induced earlier than her due date to ensure that, once the baby was full-term he could come out safely. While Ally was in labor, the baby was monitored the entire time. It was reassuring to see the lines indicating the fetal heart rate throughout her contractions. Once Ally knew that the nurses were making sure the baby was okay, she was able to shift her focus to her hypnobirthing techniques. She slowed her breath, relaxed her own heart rate, and let her body tell her when it was time to push. It wasn't until she was gripping Jack's hand as she bore down that she truly let herself believe she was actually going to have a baby. When he came out, it wasn't the first time that Ally had laid her eyes on a beautiful baby she had made—but it was the first time she heard the sound of her baby's cry.

Ally threw her head back and let her own tears flow. She let out a breath she had been holding for months. As she and Jack held their baby, it was impossible to look at him without seeing Zsazsa, too—and this brought them joy. She was part of the story that got them to this very moment: the moment they had waited for, for a very long time.

Chapter Thirteen

Jessie

Resilience was built into Jessie's constitution: she was hard-wired to be adaptable to sudden changes. This part of her personality made her talented at her job. She was the head of marketing and a product manager at an advertising agency. Her job required her to be a creative and flexible leader. She could sit with a team of people and come up with a fantastic, detailed campaign for a product, only to hear the client ask for a completely new idea. Jessie wouldn't waste any time being upset—she just moved forward.

Jessie met Cole when he was working for one of her firm's clients. He was handsome and charismatic, but also nice, which—in her experience—didn't usually follow those other two traits, at least not in her line of work. As a woman with a title next to her name, she was used to having to raise her volume to be heard at work. Early on, she learned that, when she shared an idea at a meeting, if a man just repeated it louder, he would be the one to get credit for it. She was used to dealing with men like that—so when Cole communicated respectfully and kindly while looking her in the eyes, she listened. They were able to work together on a project without any major disagreements, their teams giving and taking each other's ideas. When the project was completed, there was a celebratory dinner, and at the end of the night, Cole asked Jessie if she would like to see him again. She did.

Jessie and Cole dated for a few years, and as they fell in love with good food, travel, and adventure, they fell in love with each other. They got married surrounded by their friends, family, and coworkers, committed to continuing the partnership that worked so well both in and out of the office.

For their honeymoon, Cole and Jessie took off a few weeks to travel; they went to Thailand to enjoy a mixture of sightseeing and relaxing on the beach. They explored Bangkok—from the Grand Palace with its mystical Wat Phra Kaew to the beaches of Pattaya. At dinner together, as their trip was coming to an end, they faced each other across the table and talked about the future. They wanted more time to be together to travel, be spontaneous, and live as a married couple. They agreed that they both wanted children, but they wanted to wait a few more years.

Jessie was thirty-six when she and Cole decided to start trying to conceive a baby. After trying unsuccessfully for close to a year, Jessie went to see a fertility doctor, who explained all of the different treatment options to her and Cole. They learned about intrauterine insemination or IUI. The doctor suggested they try that first, and if that didn't work, the next step would be in vitro fertilization, or IVF.

After their first appointment, Jessie and Cole went home and tried to process everything they had learned. The price of an appointment with the fertility doctor itself was high, and each treatment cost even more. Together, they decided it was worth it—they would put everything on a credit card and figure it out later. Over the next several years Jessie tried nine rounds of IUI and three attempts with IVF, all ending unsuccessfully.

At this point, the doctor suggested that Jessie and Cole look into using a donor egg. That way, Jessie could still experience pregnancy. Jessie, however, decided it was time to look into adoption. Jessie herself was adopted, and it seemed like the obvious next step for them. If there was a baby that needed a home, she and Cole were ready to provide one.

They registered with an adoption agency, opted for open adoption, and then waited to be matched with a birth mother. When Jessie was born, adoptions were private, making it so challenging to find out any information about her birth mother. She wanted her child to be able to know their birth parents and be as involved in her child's life as they wanted to be. Jessie and Cole prepared themselves to start the waiting game again when, surprisingly, the agency notified them that they were matched with a birth mother. Everything about this adoption seemed meant to be: the birth mother was going to be delivering the baby in the very same hospital where Jessie was born. Jessie was born in Iowa but raised outside of Chicago. She and Cole lived in Seattle, and—just by chance—this baby would be born in the same part of Iowa where Jessie was born.

Jessie and Cole talked to the birth mother on the phone, flew out to meet her, and even attended a few doctor appointments with her. The woman learned that the baby was going to be a girl, and when Jessie and Cole found out that they would have a daughter, they were overjoyed. In the last few weeks before the due date, Jessie and Cole flew out to Iowa to stay and wait for the delivery. They visited the birth mother, talked to her belly, playfully introduced themselves to the baby, and even felt the baby kick.

When labor began, Jessie and Cole were right there in the delivery room with her. After the baby was born, the umbilical cord was cut, the baby was cleaned up, and soon after she was handed to Jessie. Cole wrapped his arms around Jessie—and at that moment, after waiting for over three years, they became a family. They left the hospital that night to allow the birth mother and baby to rest and recover before they could take their daughter back home to Seattle.

The next morning, as Cole and Jessie were preparing to go back to the hospital, they got a phone call from the adoption agency: the birth mother had decided to keep the baby. They couldn't believe what they were hearing. Jessie had heard of this happening and knew it was a possibility, but they had gotten this far, held their baby, and were about to take her home. Jessie tried to steady herself as the hotel room spun. She looked around, her stomach nauseous from the gut punch she felt.

"I can't believe this," she cried.

Cole was stunned, and they both wanted answers. Jessie had spent many sleepless nights reading about adoption. She knew that the birth parent had to sign the termination of parental rights and that she had up to seventy-two hours to sign them. Once that paperwork is signed, the baby will legally belong to the adopted parents. Jessie remembered reading that there was about a five percent chance of the mother changing her mind once the baby was born—she figured that the chances of it happening to them were slim. All of their communication with the birth mother and meeting the baby they thought was their little girl had eased Jessie's mind, yet here they were.

"What are we supposed to do now?" she asked. "We were supposed to go back to the hospital and fly home with our baby." Cole stopped pacing circles around the room and wrapped his arms around Jessie.

"I know. I know," said Cole as they held each other. They suddenly couldn't get out of Iowa fast enough. After catching their breath, they called the agency back to ask more questions. Jessie and Cole sat side-by-side, listening to the ringing phone through the speaker on her cell. Both mother and baby had tested positive for cocaine that morning, they learned. The birth mom had also decided that the baby looked like her boyfriend, and so she wanted to keep her and stay together. The more Jessie and Cole listened, the more they realized it was really over.

"Listen you guys, I am so sorry this happened," said their agent. "I suggest you get your names back on the adoption list as soon as possible and try again."

They hung up and began to pack their bags. Jessie stared at her diaper bag, diapers, and the baby clothes that she had carefully chosen for her baby to wear home. She froze, unsure if she should pack them and bring them back home or just leave them in the hotel room. Jessie resented the agent suggesting that they "just try again," but she stuffed everything into her suitcase anyway. Maybe one day, she could fathom the idea of going through something like this again—but not yet. She and Cole flew back home to Seattle without a baby. When they got home, all they saw were reminders of what they didn't have. There was a beautiful nursery set up, but no baby.

In time, Cole and Jessie put their names back on the adoption list. They knew it could take months. It was like dating: they had a profile page setup that explained what type of adoption they were looking for, and then a birth mother who was open to the same type of adoption policy would read through all of the profiles of possible prospective parents. It could take months, even years to get chosen.

They got an email sooner than expected from a woman who thought they would be a good match. Her name was Lily, and she was early on in her pregnancy. Jessie and Cole were hesitant to inquire more because going through the process with this woman for the rest of her pregnancy could set them back another year if she changed her mind. She was only three months along—which meant they could invest in this baby all over again, and at any point, they could lose this baby too.

Jessie decided to take the initial phone interview with Lily, and they ended up talking on the phone for close to two hours. When Jessie talked to Cole afterward, she explained that they should try to make it work with Lily—even if it doesn't work out that her baby becomes theirs, Jessie felt a real connection with Lily. Regardless of the outcome, Jessie believed that Lily was going to remain in their life.

Cole and Jessie met with Lily in Oregon and supported her through her pregnancy. Once again, they were in the room when Lily went into labor and gave birth. It was a boy, and when Lily handed him to Jessie, she said "Meet your mama, little one."

Jessie and Cole could feel how different this time was. Lily really wanted this baby to have parents who could care for him in a way that she knew she wasn't ready to do. They named him Parker, and when he was ready to leave the hospital and all the paperwork was signed, Parker flew home to Seattle with his parents: Jessie and Cole.

Jessie, Cole, and Parker stayed in touch with Lily. The family went to visit her a few times during Parker's first year, and each time, their relationship grew stronger. Lily felt like family to Jessie, and it was important to her that Parker knew his birth mother. Jessie met her own birth mother for the first time when Jessie was thirty, and it wasn't for lack of trying. She wished she could have had a relationship with her before then, but both she and her mother were grateful to be making up for the lost time.

Both Lily and Jessie's birth mothers had similar reasons for needing to put their babies up for adoption: both were young when they got pregnant, and their lives didn't lend themselves to raising a child. Lily always felt that Parker was put on this earth to complete someone else's family. She made it easy for them all to spend time together. Lily's extended family was supportive, too, and everyone enjoyed meeting and welcoming Parker. Jessie's adoptive mom had passed away when she was still a child, so having her birth mother return to her life as an adult was a bonus. Her birth mother was thrilled to have a new grandchild, and everyone was committed to staying in each other's lives.

Jessie knew, more than anyone, that—no matter how much you are loved, no matter how much you have in your life—being adopted comes with feelings of abandonment. She had a great relationship with her adoptive parents before her mother passed away, and still, there was always this feeling that someone had rejected her. When Parker was old enough to understand adoption and ask questions, Jessie could recognize the look in his eyes when he asked why Lily couldn't raise him. Jessie held her son on her lap on the edge of his bed before he went to sleep.

"Lily wasn't ready to be a mommy, but she wanted you to have a mommy and daddy who were ready for you and who love you very much, and that is how we became a family," Jessie said. She started to notice as Parker asked more and more questions, and she decided that he needed a sibling to feel less alone with the weight of his concerns.

When she told Cole what she had decided, he was completely thrown. "I thought we were one and done," he said.

Jessie explained her thinking, and although Cole understood the emotional component, he could not yet understand how a second child would work logistically. Jessie wanted to get pregnant using an egg donor this time since they had such a difficult time with adoption. She knew at this point she couldn't conceive on their own, but they could have more control over the situation if they used a donor egg and Cole's sperm.

"Hang on, Jessie," Cole said. "When did you decide you wanted to get pregnant—and how are we supposed to pay for all of this again?" They were already able to take Parker to Paris with them just on credit-card miles, thanks to putting all of their fertility and then adoption costs on airline credit cards. They had a long way to go before they would be able to pay those bills.

Jessie had done her homework, though; she had a well-researched response to every concern Cole had. She had applied to be part of a clinical study that would reduce the costs of their fertility treatments significantly. From there, she wrote out what the remaining costs could come to, made a timeline for planning purposes, and even added information on how it would benefit Parker developmentally to have a sibling. She handed her findings to Cole, who took the papers to review them—but he knew that, if his wife had gotten to the point of finding hard evidence, her mind was made up.

"You made a persuasive essay on having a second child?" he asked.

"I just put some information down. You don't have to say anything now, just think about it," she said.

Jessie's points were convincing—Cole just needed a bit of time to wrap his head around the idea. Within a few months, they were back in her fertility doctor's office. Jessie had an exam to check her uterine lining was thick enough to allow for implantation, and thankfully, she was in good shape for them to take the next steps. They learned all about the process of using an egg donor. Egg donors went through very thorough screenings for a clean bill of health. They went through blood tests to scan for genetic carrier mutations, diseases, and any overall health issues. Once their health is cleared, donors' follicles are examined to ensure that there are a good number of healthy eggs for retrieval. When all of these boxes are checked, the egg donor is registered and the prospective parents can sort through the ages of the donors, physical appearance details, and their educational backgrounds.

Cole and Jessie narrowed down their search to three egg donors. When they presented their choices to their doctor, his response sounded like he was reading them a passage from "Goldilocks and The Three Bears." One was too young, he said, one was too old, and one was just right. They went with the match that the doctor recommended and began the egg retrieval process. They signed paperwork and agreed on payment, and the donor was set to come in daily for hormones to stimulate egg production. She came for the first few days—and then didn't show up. The fertility clinic called to remind the donor that she missed an appointment but got her voicemail. On the next scheduled appointment, she didn't show up again. She never returned to the clinic, and now Cole and Jessie would have to start the process all over again.

They wanted to use a thirty-one-year-old donor next, their "older" donor, but the doctor recommended they go with the younger donor to increase their odds of success. The idea of spending more money and time only to come up short again wasn't something they wanted to do, so they heeded the doctor's advice and waited for the young donor to sign her paperwork and get cleared for egg retrieval.

After a few weeks of waiting for her ovulation to begin, the doctor discovered that, at some point in the process, the donor had become pregnant and was no longer able to participate. Three options became one last option. Cole and Jessie began the process all over again, this time with the donor they originally wanted, the thirty-one-year-old. More time passed to prepare paperwork, hormones, and egg retrieval before they finally had the eggs to fertilize. Cole contributed his sperm and the embryo was made.

Jessie went in to have IVF so that she could become pregnant, but when her doctor did an examination, he found that her uterus lining was thinner than he had originally thought. He no longer believed that she was a good candidate for pregnancy and suggested that they find a surrogate. Jessie and Cole went home that day with the all-too-familiar feeling of getting the short end of the stick.

"Do you want to stop?" Cole asked Jessie on the drive home. "If at any point you want to call it quits, you can. Lord knows you have been through a lot."

"We have been through a lot," she agreed. "Thankfully, I am not going through this shit alone. I might have gone insane if you weren't here for all this—no one would actually believe how many hurdles we have jumped through."

"Yeah, it's a lot," Cole said.

"Do you want to stop?" Jessie asked.

"I'm not the one who just got told that I won't be able to get pregnant. I already knew I couldn't get pregnant when I woke up this morning," Cole said. Jessie punched him in the arm playfully. She appreciated his humor, even though she didn't have any energy left to laugh. She mustered up a smirk before starting to cry.

"I don't know what to do now," she said. "We went this far and finally have frozen embryos that could very likely be our next child, but now my uterus has turned on me."

Jessie felt like she had just been dumped. She was sitting right next to her husband, who very much loved her—this feeling didn't come from him, but from the sting of constant rejection. She was no stranger to this feeling of loss—she had a lot of practice from the moment she was born. Her mind traveled through time. She remembered when she learned she was adopted; once she was old enough to understand what being adopted meant, she'd had this very same feeling. She remembered when her mother passed away—she'd felt this same inability to take a deep breath. When she moved to Seattle with a new roommate who turned out to be a nightmare, Jessie had to pack up and start all over again in a new apartment. After she moved a second time, she sat in her small apartment, looking out at a city full of people and feeling so alone. She had not only survived all of these hardships—she'd kept a stiff upper lip and come out the other side even stronger.

There is only so much trauma one person can take, though. As she and Cole drove home, Jessie looked out of the window at people pushing baby strollers while holding their toddler's hands and wanting to scream. No matter how many people she looked at, all she could see were families.

Jessie shut her eyes, felt the seat support her back, and reached for Cole's hand. She wasn't alone, and although she knew Cole would take the cue from her on how to move forward, they were already a family—with or without a new baby. Jessie's nature was to problem-solve five seconds before a problem arose, but infertility, adoption, egg donors, and surrogacy forced her to learn that she had little control. That night, she chose to actively not make any decisions about their future yet. She and Cole put Parker to bed that night, poured some wine, and let the day float away. They both fell asleep easily, but Jessie woke up throughout the night in her dreams. She dreamt that she had gone back to the doctor, and he'd discovered that her uterus was actually fine; they decided to give IVF a try, and she got pregnant.

Jessie woke up with a harsh reminder of how untrue that dream was, upset with her subconscious for playing tricks on her. She and Cole knew they were only left with two choices: either they didn't use the frozen embryos or they tried to find a surrogate to carry a baby for them. If they chose to not use the embryos, they would have to destroy them or pay for them to remain frozen. Neither of them was ready to even consider either of those options yet. If they used a surrogate, they would have to go through a whole new search for a healthy, trustworthy person—and they both knew too well how hard that could be.

Jessie did her best to focus her energy on her work projects. She loved working with people and creating new ideas for marketing, as well as the challenge of delivering to the clients exactly what they had in mind, seeing their faces as everything came together successfully. She welcomed the distraction from focusing on the next steps of having a baby.

At this time, Jessie was working on a campaign for the Children's Aid Society, an organization she believed in passionately. In her twenties, she had volunteered for them and was paired up with a nine-year-old named Vanessa. For the first year, Jessie would spend one afternoon a month with Vanessa doing crafts or going to the park together. As Vanessa grew up, Jessie remained a positive influence on her life. Jessie valued her relationship with Vanessa and was honored to be there to listen when she needed to talk or to give her advice if Vanessa asked. Collaborating with the Children's Aid Society was a full-circle project for Jessie; she was happy to give back to a wonderful organization that offered so much to children. Her company was working with them for a greatly reduced fee because they were a nonprofit organization—Jessie advocating for them had made this collaboration possible.

One day after work, she decided to call Vanessa to say hello. They talked every few months and were overdue to catch up. Vanessa was in her late twenties with two kids of her own now, and Parker loved it when they got together to play. They planned to get together that weekend with the kids.

That Sunday, as the kids played, Vanessa and Jessie talked. Jessie told her about the campaign she was working on. They started to reminisce about when they first met and how shy Vanessa had been. They laughed about how outgoing she had become. As the conversation went on, Jessie confided in Vanessa and told her how challenging her path to motherhood had been. She filled her in on all the donor drama—how they'd finally created embryos and now they had to figure out what to do next. Jessie explained that, if they wanted to move forward, they would have to find a surrogate to carry a baby for them.

"So, after an interesting and bizarre ride, we have arrived at this new fork in the road," Jessie said.

"I would totally have a baby for you," Vanessa said. Jessie looked up at her, unsure that she'd heard her right.

"That is a very kind gesture—thank you for saying that," Jessie said. It was sweet of Vanessa to offer, but knowing how complicated everything had already gotten, it was very likely that this too would not work out. Even Vanessa's offering was monumental. Jessie wasn't sure if she really meant it, or if she'd said it because it was the nicest thing anyone could offer her at that moment. It was all too overwhelming for Jessie to process, so she changed the subject.

Parker, now four, ran up to them, asking for a snack. Jessie reached into her bag and pulled out a little tin snack container, opening it to give Parker a few graham crackers. Vanessa's kids then asked her for crackers, too. Vanessa's kids wanted the graham crackers, and Parker wanted the Ritz crackers that Vanessa's kids had. Without fail, this happens every time children have snacks together.

"Maybe you can make my kids dinner tonight, Jessie, since they will only eat something new when it comes from you," Vanessa joked.

"We should try just swapping them out for the night and see if they are willing to eat actual food at someone else's house—although, I think it only works if other people make the food look better than the thing they are eating," said Jessie.

"Good point," Vanessa said, laughing. "We will just have to get together more often."

"Yes," Jessie agreed. "Next time, we can set up a salad bar and see what vegetables they can get each other to eat."

As they packed up to go, Jessie's mind wandered back to what Vanessa had said. Would she really go through a pregnancy for someone else? She had gone through it twice before, so she knew how big of a commitment this would be—was she really willing to go through with it again? Saying it in passing and being pregnant for nine months, going through labor and delivery, and then giving the baby over were two very different things. Jessie didn't want to go home wondering if Vanessa meant what she said, so she actually asked Vanessa before she left.

"Did you mean what you said about having a baby for us?"

"I mean it. I would one hundred percent have a baby for you," Vanessa answered without hesitation.

Jessie went home and shared the news with Cole. He was equally as shocked by Vanessa's offer, and they both agreed that, if she was willing, they should take her up on her offer. They went forward with more medical testing and paperwork; about a month after Vanessa first offered, Jessie and Cole's doctor prepared to implant an embryo into Vanessa's uterus. The doctor suggested that, since there was more than one embryo that looked promising, they implant two to increase the odds of success. Jessie and Cole were self-described as twin-averse and requested that the doctor just transfer the most promising embryo, in the hopes that they would get one healthy baby. One embryo was implanted and, a few weeks later, the phone call Jessie and Cole had waited for finally came. Vanessa was pregnant—they were pregnant—and they were going to have a baby.

When they went in with Vanessa for her first ultrasound, the three of them looked at the screen for the baby. Before their eyes could register what they were seeing, they all heard not one heartbeat, but two. They could try to avoid twins all they wanted, but the egg had split, and they would be having identical babies.

Cole's eyes widened as he looked to the technician for confirmation. "Twins?"

"Yes, looks like you have got two in there," the technician explained as he pointed out the little lives growing inside Vanessa. Jessie and Cole were shocked and worried about how they would manage twins, but they were also overjoyed to see that the surrogacy had worked. They went from having one child to being the parents of three.

Despite their joy, Jessie worried about Cole. It had taken some convincing to agree to try for a second baby, and now their family would have three kids. They went home, and Cole reassured Jessie that they would figure out how to make it all work.

Jessie and Cole chose to keep their entire process of becoming a family open and transparent. Parker knew his birth parents and their extended families. These twins would know who their biological mother was as well who carried them, and all three of them would know just how hard their parents worked to get them here.

The twins turned out to be identical twin boys, which Parker was thrilled about. Jessie held her two new baby boys in her arms to introduce them to Parker. As she took in her three boys, she realized that, for all the loss she experienced and the disappointments she faced, what she'd gained was worth so much more than all the hardships.

Chapter Fourteen

Atif

B y the time Atif was nine years old, he had lived in four different countries. His father was Pakistani, and his mother was from Jordan. His
father's job took them to Beirut for a few years, America for some, Saudi
Arabia, and eventually London, where Atif grew up. His earliest memories
of his childhood were set in London, and he grew to love living there.

After finishing college, Atif traveled a bit before working in San Francisco
in his mid-twenties. It was the first time he lived in a different country than
his family. He was no stranger to travel and hoped to move around a few more
times before settling in one place. In SF, he worked as a creative director for
a digital publication, had a nice apartment, and enjoyed being in a new city.

Atif had known he was gay for a long time—but until he arrived in San
Francisco, he hadn't dated any men. Once settled in his job, he registered with
a gay social network that connected him to other people who lived in the Bay
Area. He dated a few people over a few years, nothing serious, and none of
the relationships lasted more than a few months, but he felt himself.

Shortly after Atif turned thirty, he stumbled on Nicholas' profile. Atif
thought he was attractive right away, and when he began reading more about
him, Atif became more interested in meeting Nicholas. He reached out
online; they exchanged a few messages, then spoke on the phone a couple of
times before making plans to meet.

It turned out their jobs were one building away from each other, and on the Wednesday before they planned on getting drinks, they saw each other while getting a coffee between their offices. It was an awkward, but friendly first meeting: Atif was with co-workers, and Nicholas didn't know what to say if they were asked how they knew each other, so they just smiled and said hello. Atif was happy when they finally did go out, and the awkwardness paled in comparison to the chemistry they had. They spent a few months dating and both realized early on it felt more serious than their previous relationships.

As they grew closer, one issue grew bigger between them: Atif hadn't come out to his parents. They were on the more conservative side, and Atif didn't feel like they would welcome his news. Nicholas had grown up near San Francisco, and his mother said she knew Nicholas was gay from a young age—she was just waiting for him to tell her when he was ready. Their experiences growing up were polar opposites, yet the life they were living together was so intertwined and connected.

When Nicholas got a job offer in Australia, he let Atif know that he was thinking of taking it.

"I love you and want to be with you, but you need to figure out your situation with your family. Maybe a little time apart will do us some good," Nicholas said

"So you're giving me the 'break up for now' talk that is contingent on me talking to my parents?" Atif joked. He knew that Nicholas was right, but it was painful to think of taking time apart and challenging to imagine coming out to his parents. Nicholas's job in Australia was scheduled to last for six weeks—and while Nicholas was gone, Atif could regroup and make a plan. He knew he wanted to be with Nicholas, and he was ready to be honest about who he was with his family.

Nicholas's job went from six weeks to a few months. When it became clear that sustaining their relationship with this much distance wasn't feasible, Nicholas and Atif broke up. It wasn't spoken aloud that Atif hadn't talked to his parents yet—but it didn't need to be. Nicholas knew that Atif would tell him once it happened, and since they hadn't had that conversation yet, he decided to stay in Australia and continue with the job extension that was offered. They spent six months apart, and Atif missed Nicholas terribly—but Atif wanted the conversation with his parents to happen when he was ready, not just to keep his relationship with Nicholas intact.

When Atif finally decided it was time to come out to his parents, he wrote them a letter and mailed it to their house. He wanted to make sure he could say everything he wanted them to know and was afraid that, if he did it in person, he might not be able to do it. After the letter arrived, Atif never spoke about his sexuality in person with his parents, but he did call them to make sure they had received the letter. They acknowledged that they did but chose not to say much else. The inner conflict Atif had felt about how his parents would react turned out to be warranted: they basically chose to ignore what he had to say. They didn't cut him out of their lives or plead with him—they just never talked about his sexuality with him after getting the letter.

It took time to come to terms with his parents' response, yet Atif felt lighter. He began to breathe a bit easier knowing his life wasn't a secret anymore. Atif reached out to Nicholas and told him everything that had happened. He asked if they could see each other, and they planned to meet in New York. They continued to live in different cities for a few more months, but after this visit, they were together again. They never went a few weeks without meeting somewhere in the world.

When they finally lived in the same city together, Atif wanted his parents to know about Nicholas; it was one thing to come out to them, but a whole other reality when there was actually a real person attached. When Atif introduced Nicholas to his parents, they were friendly, kind, and—as he expected—uncomfortable, but Atif and Nicholas agreed the meeting could be considered successful. Atif and Nicholas moved in together and eventually got married. They didn't have a big ceremony or celebration—they just wanted to be together.

Early on in their relationship, Atif and Nicholas learned that they were on the same page about wanting to have children. They began to talk about parenthood with more certainty about six months after moving in together. Neither one of them had felt the need for those children to be biologically theirs, so they began researching adoption. They learned about a private adoption facilitator run by attorneys who started their company with the goal of helping birth mothers find parents in a manner that felt respectful and considerate. There were many challenges that came along with adoptions, and this group of lawyers prioritized what they believed was fair for both parties.

From the moment Nicholas and Atif seemed serious about each other, Nicholas' mother reminded them that she was waiting for a grandchild—so they let her know that they were beginning the process of adoption as soon as they got started. Atif didn't share any of the news with his parents until they were paired with a baby.

The agency found a match for Atif and Nicholas, and they were introduced to a birth mother named Brielle. Paperwork was drafted for an open adoption. Brielle was no longer involved with the biological father, so Nicholas and Atif's interactions were mainly with her and the attorneys. Atif and Nicholas accompanied Brielle to a few doctors' appointments and, as the birth grew closer, they began to wrap their minds around the possibility that they could become parents very soon.

Atif let his parents know that he and Nicholas were in the process of adopting a baby. They didn't say very much that day, but they did say that they recognized that this baby would be their grandchild. To Atif and Nicholas, that was the most important part of what they had hoped to get from sharing their news with Atif's parents. With everyone in their inner circle now aware of their adoption, it became more and more real to Nicholas and Atif. They began to make space for the baby in their home. They put together a nursery. They purchased diapers and a car seat—and they waited.

Adoption complications are common: there are many steps, loopholes, and hurdles to traverse before an adoption is completed successfully. Atif and Nicholas were not in the dark about these possible obstacles. They had heard the many stories of birth mothers who changed their minds after seeing their child, deciding to keep their baby. They had heard of family members, boyfriends, and friends coming into the picture once a baby is born and adoptive parents losing their right to a child they thought was theirs. When Atif and Nicholas finally got the call that Brielle was in labor, all of these possibilities swam around in their minds.

Atif and Nicholas met Brielle at the hospital, where she gave birth to a healthy baby boy. He was handed to Atif and Nicholas by the nurses. Brielle, exhausted, smiled and looked pleased to see the baby in their arms. Nicholas and Atif spent the day holding the baby, staring at him, biding their time, and holding out hope that he would become their son.

The final step in an adoption is the completion of a consent-to-adopt form, which needs to be filled out by the birth mother once she and the child are released from the hospital. By design, the form cannot be signed until the birth mother is strong enough and of clear enough mind after giving birth, in order to ensure that she understands what she is signing. The type of birth a birth mother has gone through determines how many days it could take to get signed. If the mother had a Cesarean section, was given pain medication, or otherwise needs time to heal in the hospital, those days are taken into account. Once the form is signed, it needs two business days to be approved. Depending on the day of the week, a weekend or holiday could further delay this process.

Once their adoption was finalized, Atif and Nicholas named their son Nathaniel. When they brought him home from the hospital, they walked him around their house, introducing him to his new surroundings. They looked at him and at each other celebrating their new family, gratefully beginning sleepless nights, diaper changing, and round-the-clock feedings. Their lives were turned inside out but in the best possible way: they had become parents. Nathaniel was surrounded by love. Not just his fathers, but his grandparents and extended family—even Atif's parents—were all so pleased to welcome him.

The open adoption agreement between Atif, Nicholas, and Brielle delineated that they would share photos with Brielle from time to time and have a visit about once a year. Atif, Nicholas, Nathaniel, and Brielle went out to lunch together when Nathaniel was about eighteen months old. They exchanged pleasantries and the energy at the table was friendly. Nathaniel was shy around Brielle, and Brielle was pleasant, but not overly engaged or interested in Nathaniel—which was just fine with Atif and Nicholas.

"I have some news that I wanted to tell you guys," Brielle said, in between bites of her turkey club. "I am pregnant again, and I am wondering if you would be interested in adopting this baby as well."

Atif put down his fork and picked up his napkin to wipe his face—and to cover his mouth, in case it was hanging open in surprise. Both he and Nicholas had always wanted a second child, but it never occurred to them that it could be from the same birth mother...or that it would be proposed as a possibility to them while sitting and having lunch!

"First of all, congratulations Brielle, that's big news," Nicholas said, realizing that wishing her congratulations felt odd in light of her adoption offer. He wasn't sure what to say next. "Let Atif and I discuss this and think it over. Thank you for thinking of us," Nicholas managed to get out.

"Do you know how far along you are? Or when the due date is?" Atif asked.

"I am about five months along," Brielle responded. Atif and Nicholas could tell that she wasn't really sure about her offer, so they didn't press with any other questions. Instead, they finished their lunch, eager to return to their car and discuss this new turn of events.

Adopting Brielle's new baby would be ideal for Atif and Nicholas. This child had a different biological father, but it would still be Nathanial's biological half-sibling. They had already gone through this process with Brielle, so they were familiar with her and her family. Atif and Nicholas wanted a second child and, without starting the search all over again, this opportunity simply came to them. They didn't take long to decide; they called Brielle and then the agency to let them know they wanted to move forward with the adoption.

For a successful adoption, a birth mother is required to attend all of her doctor appointments. When Atif and Nicholas were alerted that Brielle had missed one, they scheduled another lunch with her. They didn't want to be confrontational, but they felt that they should check in and see how she was feeling. On the day of the lunch, Atif and Nicholas waited for Brielle at the restaurant—but she never showed up. They called her, left her a message, and texted her, asking her to just let them know she was okay, but her communication stopped. They didn't hear from her for several weeks.

Atif and Nicholas knew that Brielle had struggled with drug use in the past. Brielle's mother Vicky finally reached out to them and confirmed their fears—Brielle had started using again. Vicky thanked them for adopting Nathaniel and pleaded with them to not give up on this adoption. Vicky had already raised another of Brielle's children before Brielle had Nathaniel, and she was so grateful that Atif and Nicholas were going to adopt this baby, too.

The situation put Atif and Nicholas in a most vulnerable position. They wanted to proceed with the adoption, but they worried about the health of Brielle and the baby. They didn't know how much Brielle was using and hoped for the best as the pregnancy went on. When Vicky let Atif and Nicholas know Brielle was getting close to the end of the pregnancy, they once again prepared their home to bring in a new baby.

The day the call arrived that Brielle was in labor, Atif and Nicholas made care arrangements for Nathaniel. "When Daddy and I come back and get you, you are going to be a big brother to a new baby," Nicholas said as he hugged Nathaniel. Atif put his arm around Nicholas and looked at their son. As hard as this all was, it had brought Nathaniel to them, and that was enough of a reminder to keep moving forward.

When they got to the hospital, Vicky greeted them, taking another opportunity to thank them profusely for adopting the baby. Brielle, however, was not quite as engaging with them as she had been in the past. She said hello but didn't maintain eye contact. She seemed uncomfortable—but she was in labor, so Atif and Nicholas pushed aside their concerns and chalked it up to labor pains.

Suddenly, a man appeared in the room, and things got awkward. Nicholas and Atif recognized him: they had ridden up in the elevator with him. This man was the biological father, and it became apparent to Nicholas and Atif that the father didn't quite understand how adoption worked. If he did, he certainly didn't understand that the baby Brielle was about to have was going to be adopted by anyone at all, let alone by Atif and Nicholas.

As the pieces started to come together for Atif and Nicholas, they recognized that the puzzle was even bigger and more complicated than they could have imagined. Their instincts on Brielle's behavior were spot-on: she was still struggling with addiction. The biological father was not on the same page as Vicky, and he wasn't quite as grateful to see Atif and Nicholas preparing to take the baby home. After some back-and-forth, Nicholas and Atif discovered that the father believed he would retain some rights to his child, including having input into the baby's name and being involved as a parent. That wasn't what was agreed upon by the agency, nor were Atif and Nicholas comfortable with that arrangement—but at that moment, Nicholas and Atif did their best to play their cards carefully. They didn't say no to his requests, but they also didn't say yes.

Vicky could see that Atif and Nicholas were concerned, and she asked the three of them to step into the hallway. "Again, I just want to say how happy I am that you two will be in this baby's life," Vicky said. "I know Brielle's friend in there thinks he wants this baby, but they are both still using."

"We are grateful for this baby too, Vicky," Atif said, nodding, unsure how to respond to the rest of what he'd learned.

"With the state of those two, this baby would end up back in my care, and I am not going to raise another one of Brielle's babies," Vicky said.

"We don't want that either," Nicholas said, attempting to keep the conversation short and to the point.

Throughout Brielle's labor, Nicholas and Atif stayed agreeable and neutral whenever the biological dad asked questions. Brielle gave birth to a baby girl who was born addicted to drugs. While at the hospital, Atif and Nicholas were taught how to care for the baby in order to help wean her off the drugs. They were told that the process of weaning her would take time. Brielle had used methadone and over the next few weeks, they would have to give the baby small doses of the drug and wean her from it gradually each day.

Despite the stress of the labor and the father's unexpected appearance, the baby was handed over to Atif and Nicholas as planned. Atif and Nicholas named her Freya. In order to keep things amicable with the birth father, they let him choose Freya's middle name: Marie.

When Freya was healthy enough to be released from the hospital, Atif and Nicholas took her home. Nathaniel met his baby sister and asked if he could hold her. After washing his hands, Nicholas helped Nathaniel sit upright on the couch with pillows around him. Atif sat down next to Nathaniel and gently placed Freya in his arms while Atif wrapped his arms around them both.

"Daddy, she is so tiny, with tiny, tiny fingers," Nathaniel said, taking in his baby sister. Atif smiled and then looked up at Nicholas, whose eyes were tearing up.

Together, Atif and Nicholas fed Freya and tended to her around the clock, doing everything they learned at the hospital to help get Freya healthy.

Brielle left the hospital on a Thursday. Her relinquishment of parental rights would not be made final until she signed her consent to adopt and the two business days for processing had passed. Atif and Nicholas cared for Freya at home for five days, after which they waited by their phones, hoping to get the call from the agency saying that Brielle signed the forms—but the call never came. They hoped that she just needed a bit more time or that processing the forms was held up for some reason. There were many scenarios that didn't end well, so they spent their days together at home trying to focus on being a family.

After having Freya for a week, Atif and Nicholas's phone finally rang. Instead of receiving the call that recognized Freya was legally theirs, the agency gave them the news that no adoptive parent with a newborn ever wants to get. The lawyer explained to them that Brielle and her boyfriend wanted to keep the baby. However, Brielle was still using, so there was no way that the baby would be put in her care. Brielle had convinced Vicky to care for the baby while she got clean. Consistently, this agency did its best to help all parties involved, and the tone in the attorney's voice revealed how truly difficult it was for him to deliver this news. He offered their office as a middle ground to return the baby.

Atif and Nicholas were given one day to surrender Freya back into Vicky's hands. There were more tears shed than words spoken between them that night. They didn't need to speak; their shared disappointment was palpable. They'd loved Freya from the moment they brought her into their world, and giving her back would leave them with an abundant supply of love without an outlet to pour it into. They thought about Nathaniel and how to explain this news to a two-year-old.

The next night, they packed Freya into the car. Filled with resentment, frustration, and sadness, they drove to the agency's office to return Freya to Vicky. They struggled with whether or not to give her all the diapers, clothes, and the car seat. If it was out of spite that they chose not to, then that spite was a small sacrifice in the grand scheme of what they did have to hand over that night.

When they walked into the quiet office building, they felt its dark emptiness. One office with a light on waited just for them.

When they walked into the office, Vicky walked up to them and began to apologize immediately. "I just want to explain that Brielle really..." she started to say.

"We are not interested in hearing what you have to say, Vicky," Atif said—and they weren't. Everything was elucidated by the phone call they had received the day before, and they didn't need or want any more explanation. They each took a moment to hold Freya, trying to find an impossible closure. They handed Freya over to Vicky and silently left the building. When they got back to the car, their tears erupted, and they held one another.

The next morning, when Nathaniel woke up and asked where Freya was, Atif and Nicholas had an answer at the ready. They had consulted with a therapist on how best to present the situation to Nathaniel and were told to be direct and keep the conversation short; Nathaniel would forget quickly because he was so young. Atif and Nicholas wouldn't but Nathaniel would.

"Freya had to go to a different home. We love her very much, but she won't be living here anymore." Atif heard himself say. Although none of the words sounded right, hearing himself say them made it all more concrete, sending a sharp wave of sadness down his spine. Much to Atif's surprise, Nathaniel seemed to accept his answer. Atif dropped off Nathaniel at daycare and tried to say goodbye as if it was a normal day.

Atif returned home to Nicholas. They had taken the day off of work to clear the house of anything that belonged to Freya: her baby gear, her crib, her bouncy seat, her swaddle blankets, her diapers. This clearing represented the second part of the therapist's advice about Nathaniel's understanding of the situation: erase any evidence in the house that she had ever been there. So Atif and Nicholas moved every baby item out of the house. When they were done, they both felt so depleted, and exhausted physically and emotionally. This was the deepest loss that either of them had ever experienced.

They went dark for three months after Freya's return to Vicky. They never spoke about her around Nathaniel, but Atif and Nicholas mourned her loss both together and separately. Each focused their energy on Nathaniel, and that quality time helped them begin to close the hole that Freya's loss had left. Atif reached out to his parents more, who began to spend more time with Nicholas and Nathaniel. It wasn't always perfect—but they loved Nathaniel, and he loved his grandparents.

One afternoon, Atif watched as his father played with his son, and Atif smiled. The joy that he felt watching them together caught him off-guard—he realized it was the first time since Freya's leaving that he felt any lightness. He let himself succumb to the moment, feeling grateful for the happiness washing over him.

One night after Nathaniel was asleep, Atif asked Nicholas what he thought of looking again for another baby. They agreed that they wanted to have another baby in their lives, even though they knew the risks of starting the process all over again. The experience they had gained from losing Freya bonded them together, ready to move forward with a new layer of armor. They began looking on the adoption agency's site for a new match.

A few months later, they got a call from the agency: a woman named Rebecca was interested in them adopting her baby. They researched the details, checked when the baby was due, and braced themselves for yet another scenario where the outcome could leave them without a baby. There was nothing that they could do to influence that possibility one way or another, so they decided to take the risk and said "yes."

Rebecca went into labor weeks earlier than expected. Atif was away on a business trip, so Nicholas was juggling work and Nathaniel solo when he got the call to come to the hospital. He called Atif in a panic.

"The baby is coming, you aren't here, and what do I do with Nathaniel? I can't take him to the hospital," Nicholas said. Atif knew exactly who to call. He hadn't shared much of the adoption details yet with his parents. Until there was a baby, he didn't really want to open up himself to any issues his parents might raise with how Atif and Nicholas became a family. He did know, though, that they loved their grandchild and would love whoever else would come to call them grandparents in the future.

"My parents can help with Nathaniel. I'll call them and call you right back," Atif said. He picked up the phone and his mother answered. As quickly as he could, he explained to them the whole situation. Without hesitation, his mother stepped up to help.

"Your father and I will be there, Atif, just calm down. It is going to be okay," his mother said.

Nicholas arrived at the hospital right before Rebecca gave birth via Cesarean. She had a healthy baby girl, and shortly after delivery, the baby was handed over to Nicholas. By the next day, Rebecca was no longer receiving pain medication and was recovering well from her C-section. Atif flew in as soon as he could and drove straight to the hospital. When he walked into the hospital room and saw Nicholas holding their baby girl, he silently prayed that this time, she would remain in their care. Atif walked over and looked at her so tightly wrapped in a hospital blanket; he opened his arms to Nicholas so that Atif could hold her.

As soon as Rebecca could be discharged from the hospital, she signed the paperwork. It was sent to the agency right away, and the baby was legally theirs a few days later. When Atif and Nicholas brought their tiny new daughter Lily home, they were greeted by Nathaniel and his grandparents.

"Come and meet your new granddaughter," Atif said as he walked over to his dad. He placed her into his father's arms as his family surrounded them.

Atif had never experienced that moment when a parent, at long last, lets their child know they respect his identity. Though it would have been nice to hear his parents say those words, he accepted that their actions speak loudly enough. Atif has his parents in his life, Atif is a part of their lives, and his parents are a part of their grandchildren's lives.

From time to time, Atif and Nicholas would wonder about Freya. They rarely heard from Brielle except for the occasional request from her for photos of Nathaniel, which they furnished without questions or comments.

When Atif watches his children play together as brother and sister, he realizes that it was the turn of all of the events, like Brielle being addicted, having to give back Freya, Rebecca choosing them, and her going into labor early, led them all together. On the occasion when Freya pops into his thoughts and he looks at Lily, he is able to feel loss and gratitude simultaneously. Had things worked out differently, he would never have gotten to know his daughter, who he can't imagine life without.

The adoption process opened Atif's eyes to the judgment so easily passed on birth mothers and their circumstances. In the past, he himself had been one to judge the choices that caused these women to choose to put their children up for adoption. His experiences taught Atif that opportunities aren't rolled out in life equally. He understood now that it was a privilege to have the options that he had in life, options that many others didn't. He was grateful to the adoption agency for always striving to do what was best for these birth mothers—grateful that these women were given a choice whether or not they wanted to raise their children. Atif knew that he and Nicholas had a family because these women had that choice. This is what connects them all in a world in which they would not otherwise have been connected.

Chapter Fifteen

Shea

Trying to become pregnant the first time was no small feat. My husband and I tried for close to a year without success. Each month my period came, adding insult to injury: it was bad enough that I wasn't pregnant, but I also had to deal with my period monthly until we could try again.

After that year, I saw a doctor, who ordered an HSG test to determine why I couldn't conceive. An hysterosalpingography (or HSG) is a procedure in which dye is injected into your fallopian tubes to identify any obstructions. Turns out, a sesame seed-sized fibroid had grown right at the opening to my uterus. My doctor scheduled surgery for the next month—but before we reached the appointment date I started feeling horrible cramping, always at night. I had never felt anything quite so painful. On the third night, my husband called the doctor, and she suggested we go to the emergency room. There, I learned that I was pregnant.

The news was bittersweet: I was happy to learn that I was actually pregnant, but the ER doctor told me that the pregnancy probably wouldn't last. A side effect of the HSG procedure is that the fallopian tubes are flushed open—which made it possible for me to get pregnant—but the fibroid was still there, which was the cause of my intense pain. The fibroid and the pregnancy were fighting for the same blood supply, and I would just have to wait it out to see which was stronger.

After a few days, I went back to my regular OB. He drew blood, which revealed that my hormone count was growing and I was still pregnant. Then he did an ultrasound, showing my husband and me both the yolk sack and the fibroid—so tiny for all the trouble they were causing me.

The pain continued for a few weeks, and so did my pregnancy. Eventually, the baby won over the fibroid: after those few painful weeks, the fibroid disappeared. I was just beginning to enjoy the idea of pregnancy in my seventh week when I began throwing up. I started with one day in the afternoon and then the next day in the morning. I bought motion sickness bands, ginger ale, sucking candies, and ice pops, but nothing helped. I began vomiting multiple times a day, and I was becoming less and less able to eat anything. There were days that, if I threw up eight times, it was a good day.

I learned that there was a name for what I was going through hyperemesis gravidarum, or HG, a complication of pregnancy that causes severe nausea, vomiting, and dehydration. It affects under two percent of pregnant women, so I guess I should consider myself a very unique and special person. There were windows of time at the end of the day when I could eat something that might stay down. Usually, it was some bland, white, starchy food like pretzels or a bagel—but even those weren't a sure bet. I tried to sip some sort of electrolyte drink as much as possible, but nothing felt good. I tried to remember a time that I actually liked food and had trouble finding any fondness for any of it. I chose to watch shows like *America's Next Top Model* which had little to no commercials for food. Seeing food would cause me to gag, and smelling it was a guarantee that I would throw up. It felt like a form of torture waking up every morning and immediately feeling so sick.

Every time I went to the doctor and shared how I was feeling, he told me that the baby was fine. He showed me the ultrasounds of this thriving little person growing inside me. He explained that the baby was taking everything it needed from me, which is why I was feeling horrible while it was doing just fine.

One day before a doctor's appointment, the nurse asked me to step on the scale. I watched her move the weight block from the one-hundred-pound notch down to the ninety-pound notch. When I saw that I weighed only ninety-three pounds I panicked. My husband mentioned it right away to the doctor, who hadn't been alarmed until he realized how much weight I had lost. The doctor phoned in a prescription for a medication that he explained would make me very tired but would help to stop the nausea. He told me that, if I could gain or at least maintain my weight through the weekend, he could keep me from having to go to the hospital for a feeding tube.

I took the medicine, and my husband asked me to choose any food that sounded appealing and he would buy it for me. The only things I could even fathom eating were frozen pizza and tater tots—but I was able to eat a bit before falling asleep. The next morning when I woke up, I didn't feel like throwing up, but I felt antsy. I couldn't sit still, in a way that I imagined Restless Leg Syndrome might feel, but I felt it everywhere.

Within a half-hour of the jitters' onset, that feeling took hold of my jaw, and I was unable to move it at all. The medication had caused lockjaw. I never thought I would prefer throwing up—but at that moment, I would have taken anything over the pain in my jaw. My husband called the doctor and told him what was happening. The doctor promised that the baby and I would be okay and that the medication would wear off. My jaw stayed locked for sixteen hours, and at the end of the day, my husband was the one throwing up from all the stress the reaction had caused.

After my jaw finally released and the soreness subsided, my husband and I returned to the doctor to check that everything was okay. The baby was totally fine through all that chaos; it even had a nice laid-back disposition, its little legs crossed as if to say "Just relaxing here, and the water is just right."

We went home that day a little worse for wear, but we felt grateful that what seemed to be a superhero baby was faring so well. I continued to be sick all the way through the sixteenth week and then had a glorious respite until the very end of my pregnancy.

I had a long labor that arrived almost two weeks past my due date, but—despite throwing up between contractions—I gave birth to a healthy baby girl. I stared at every detail of her face, marveling that she came out a fully formed little human. I couldn't believe it worked, that I had grown this beautiful little person. I fell in love with her instantly, and my husband and I were so excited to be parents. When we brought her home, we would race each other to be the first one to pick her up when she started to cry. Every milestone and every moment, we proudly soaked up. It felt like a restart button had been pressed on our lives: we'd found access to a kind of love in our hearts that we didn't know was even there until we had her.

A few years later, when many of my friends who had babies around the same time as I did started to have second children, I couldn't fathom it. I knew I wanted a second child, but I was not at all ready to go through another pregnancy. I also wanted more time as a family of three. I waited a year and decided to try again—I figured three-and-a-half years apart was a good age difference.

This time, I got pregnant right away; I got sick right away, too. Being so nauseous, getting sick, and caring for a two-and-a-half-year-old was not working very well. I had gone in to see my doctor, who gave me an ultrasound showing me my second little baby swimming around happily on the monitor. That was motivation to keep going—but the doctor said that, if the nausea got too tough in the weeks ahead, he wanted me to try an IV drip of a medicine.

I made it from the six-week appointment to the nine-week ultrasound, but my nausea felt unbearable. My husband and I got to see the baby again—but as reassuring as this was, I knew I needed help. The doctor set me up with a company that came to our house with an IV pole, a bag with a pump, and a tiny tube that I would wear daily. They taught my husband how to give me an IV drip for fluids, which I could barely look at, let alone let my husband inject into one of my veins. I never had a great experience with getting blood taken or getting an IV. No matter how calm I tried to remain during the process, there was always difficulty finding a vein. It always turned into a poke fest and over the years I began to fear it more and more. If a professional had a hard time finding a vein, how would my husband? They gave me strips to test my urine daily for hydration levels and showed me how to inject my own stomach twice daily to create a port for the anti-nausea medication.

It would take me several tries before I was brave enough to poke myself. I had to pinch and hold my skin while my other hand pushed in a small needle attached to a small plastic base. After much overthinking and numerous failed attempts, I would finally get it in—and *then* I would have to attach the top of the base to the tube that carried the medicine into my bloodstream. Fortunately, the medicine worked quite quickly, and I was able to get out of bed without getting sick. I wore the pump like a small purse over my shoulder with the tube attached to my shirt. This setup lasted for a few weeks, until the next doctor's appointment.

When I went in for my three-month ultrasound appointment, I got nervous. I wasn't sure why I worried about the baby—perhaps because I wasn't accustomed to being pregnant without throwing up. Despite having seen a healthy growing baby in the ninth week, I remained afraid of finding out bad news. I suppose on some level I was always afraid of this, felt the fear prior to every ultrasound—but on that particular morning, I looked at the sky. It was a perfect, beautiful, clear day, and I told myself that, no matter what happened at the appointment, the day would still be beautiful. If we got bad news, it didn't mean that all was lost. The sun would still shine upon us.

While waiting for the doctor to come into the room, my hands began to sweat. I told my husband I was nervous, and he tried to reassure me that everything was likely fine, playfully wondering if this baby would get his blue eyes since our daughter had my brown.

"Too bad an ultrasound can't tell you that," I said, trying to play along.

"Someone should invent that—there is definitely a market for it," he said, smiling

There was a knock on the door, and I jumped. Suddenly, the wave of nerves returned. The doctor walked in with all the obligatory greetings.

"How are you guys today?" he asked.

"I am actually feeling a little concerned—I don't know why, but I am feeling anxious," I replied, in such a direct way that I even took myself back. No one actually says "How are you?" and expects people to be truly honest, but I didn't feel up for pleasantries or chit-chat that day.

The doctor switched gears immediately and got right to business. He flipped the light switch down so that he could see the monitor clearly.

"Well, let's take a look and see," the doctor said as he moved the wand around. I didn't hear anything, so I looked carefully at the screen to see what he was seeing, searching for movement.

"Unfortunately, there isn't a heartbeat." the doctor said, but I only heard his first word— "unfortunately" was enough for me to know that my instincts were correct. As the tears started to pool in my eyes, my hands immediately went to the pump that I wore. I took the strap off my shoulder, lifted my shirt, and pulled out the port needle that had been attached to my body. There was no point in wearing it a second longer. It seemed clear to me that, when my nausea stopped, so did my baby's heartbeat.

There are many reasons why women miscarry, from not enough chromosomes developing in the fetus to too many, other sorts of abnormal fetal development, undetected medical issues, environmental hazards, and more: the list goes on and on. Sometimes it's just the random luck of the draw that causes one to miscarry. It is so much more common than we understand because so many women don't share when it happens. There are also many reasons for this secrecy, from sadness to loss, shame, the feeling of failure, and grief. The subject of miscarriage has become more transparent in recent years, but overall it is still quite taboo. Even the common practice of not sharing your pregnancy until the second trimester is designed to keep a woman from having to share her loss, should she not get out of the "shaky" first trimester.

My doctor explained to me that I had experienced something called a missed miscarriage. The baby had only made it to about eleven weeks, but I didn't exhibit any signs of miscarriage. No bleeding, no cramps—the baby just quietly ceased to grow, its tiny heart no longer beating. In my case, it seemed that the baby's heart stopped a day or two after the surge of medicine was pumped into my body. In the beginning, it was helpful to have a reason for why I wasn't going to have this baby. I wanted to be able to blame something for it. I eventually found similar cases to mine online—there was even a lawsuit against the brand of medicine, women who also had IVs and ports to pump medication into their veins, only to have it stop the beating hearts of their unborn babies.

Once I learned that the baby was gone, I wanted to get it out; I was too sad to hold on to what I knew was already gone. I was too far along and the baby was too big for me to have a D&C in my doctor's office, so the nurse in my doctor's office was kind enough to get me an appointment at the hospital the next day. When I signed in at the hospital, I saw that the name of the procedure was an abortion. I looked up at the receptionist and asked if this was a mistake. An abortion to me implies that a woman has a choice, but I didn't choose to lose this baby. The receptionist looked back at me with understanding eyes.

"I know it doesn't seem to fit what you are going through, but that is just what they call it. I am sorry," she said.

There was so much compassion coming from her that I wished I could reach over the desk and let her hug me. She seemed like the type of person who would hold me as long as I needed. Maybe she had miscarried at some point too, or just saw enough women like me come in asking the same question, or maybe she just knew what it felt like to lose a part of your life just as you were getting to know it. From the moment I got pregnant, my identity changed. Pregnancy made me feel like a mother to both my daughter and the child I was growing. When I woke up on the day of the procedure, I felt robbed of that part of my identity.

Despite our grief, my husband and I found a moment of levity in the waiting room. I asked my husband if I could name the baby Gabriel: the only boy's name we had agreed on when I was pregnant with my daughter. My husband wasn't totally in love with the name for our first child and let me know in the middle of a contraction when I was in labor. I told him that we could talk about it later, but we didn't have to, because she was a girl. Since we weren't going to be living with this baby, I thought it would be nice to name him or her the name Gabriel, since it meant angel.

"Sure, and you may as well throw in your Sailor, Clover, and Marigold too since we won't be using those next time either," my husband said.

I had put those three names high on my list of favorite choices, and he didn't quite hold them in the same regard. The way he said it made me laugh.

"Next time?" I asked.

I was worried—after all the sickness, medicine, injections, and disappointment—that my husband would be deterred from us trying again in the future. I wanted so badly to get pregnant again, but I knew it could take months to get back to the point where we could even try. I was discouraged and disheartened by all we had lost. But when my husband said "next time," it was the first time anyone acknowledged that there could be a rainbow coming after the shit storm we were currently weathering.

"Yes, we should try again. We should try one more time—but, no matter what happens, that is about all any of us can handle," he said. I didn't disagree. I wasn't sure I could go through weeks and weeks of being sick again, only to lose another baby.

It had been hard enough for me to try a second time, so I crossed my fingers that the third time would be the charm. Whatever happened, we were a team; when I felt weak my husband found strength enough for both of us. He watched our little girl and reassured me that, no matter what happened, we would be okay in the end. We would try again. Just one more time, though.

Waiting for the green light to be able to try again felt like forever, even though in reality it was less than two months. The suggested window of time to wait is three months, but my doctor gave us the go-ahead at an appointment seven weeks after my D&C. I got pregnant right away, which surprised me, given everything my body had gone through. I didn't understand how getting pregnant could come so easily while *staying* healthy while pregnant seemed a monumental task.

My husband and I decided that this time, I would tackle the pregnancy without medication. There were too many risks involved for me. The only thing my doctor insisted on was that I go into the office twice a week for an IV drip of fluid to avoid getting dehydrated.

As expected, I began getting sick around six weeks into the pregnancy. Other than getting sick at different times of the day, the severity of the vomiting was about the same. I learned that I couldn't eat one meal at night like I had when I was pregnant with my daughter; this time, if I went to sleep after eating, nausea would wake me up. The only time I could manage to get a bit of food down was before 10:30 in the morning. After that, all bets were off. I also couldn't seem to get out of bed after 1:00 PM without getting sick. My daughter would come home from preschool around two and crawl into bed with me. I loved her and wanted to hold her—but everything and everyone smelt bad to me. I felt awful that holding my own child could make me sick. We came up with a routine that worked; eventually, she would come home and lie on the bed next to me after changing from school.

It wasn't perfect, but it was better. We would watch *Dora The Explorer"* together, which she loved and, to this day, reminds me of being pregnant and sick.

I would read her books and we would play games from the bed. It was all I could muster as her mother, and she seemed grateful for what time I could give her. As hard as it was on me, this change strengthened my daughter's relationship with my husband. Up until that point, she was pretty much a mama's girl. This experience gave them a chance to bond and spend time together. Even though I look back at the time with some horrible memories, for my husband it was a very special time as a father.

At around sixteen weeks, I started to feel better and could keep down small meals. I took pride and pleasure in watching my belly grow bigger, but there was a part of me that could not rest easy until I held this baby in my arms. I held my breath each time I had a doctor's appointment and got an ultrasound. Whenever I saw the heartbeat and movement on the monitor, I could finally exhale.

Unlike the first pregnancy, when we wanted to be surprised by the gender, we decided to find out this time. We wanted some part of it to still be a surprise, though, and we hadn't told our daughter yet that I was pregnant. My friend wanted to be in on the plan on how to tell her, so we all decided that the doctor would determine the gender and put it into an envelope, and then my friend would meet me at the appointment to look at the "verdict." She then gave us a little wrapped box with a tiny doll inside that was either male or female. We took the box from her, unopened, and picked up our daughter from preschool. Once we arrived home, we sat down on a blanket together.

"Sweet girl, we want to tell you some news. Mommy has a baby in her belly," my husband explained.

"You are going to be a big sister," I chimed in.

"What is it? A boy or a girl?" our three-year-old asked.

"We don't know. You tell us." I said as we handed her the tiny box. She un-wrapped it and pulled out a miniature gray bunny rabbit with a blue lace diaper on.

"Wow!" said my husband.

"It's a girl!" said my daughter.

"Wait, what is it?" I asked.

My daughter decided she wanted a girl—and since the rabbit was so pretty, and blue was one of her favorite colors, she decided I was having a girl. My husband understood it was a boy, but I was confused, so I dug into my bag to see what the doctor wrote in the envelope, just to be sure. It was a boy indeed—and since we knew that at three one's temperament can be quite fragile, we decided not to push the idea of a brother on her just then. That night before she went to bed, I read her a story and tucked her in.

"Mommy, it's a boy, isn't it?" she asked as I stood in her doorway.

"Yes, sweetness. It's a boy," I answered.

As we all prepared to welcome this new baby into our lives, my husband and I discussed names. We decided that whatever name we came up with would be kept between us. Coming up with a boy's name the first time was so challenging, and we had never fully agreed on one. This time we both landed on one we fell in love with.

One day, I called a dear friend as I sat parked outside my daughter's preschool, waiting to pick her up. It had been some time since we had talked, and I told her about naming the baby we had lost Gabriel. This friend loved reading cards for people. She didn't read tarot cards or claim to read the future; she was a spiritual person who had these decks of cards with different themes. They were called Oracle cards. Some were based on the elements, others had quotes, and the one she had picked that day was about angels. She read a card to me about the angel Gabriel and how he represented strength, and then she pulled another card to read to me. She knew I was pregnant again, and she wished that reading me these cards would provide me with some hope as I moved forward with my pregnancy.

I held back my reaction to my friend over the phone. I didn't want to cry happy or sad tears, but I was stunned. I don't typically give much weight to these kinds of readings. I enjoy them and find them interesting—but I don't necessarily believe in them. I like the idea of magical thinking, but I don't really believe in magic. I do believe, though, that there are moments when people's intuition leads to truth and that certain situations just line up with perfect synchronicity. That is how I felt after this reading from my friend. I thanked her for telling me all about the angels and got off the phone to pick up my little girl.

I hadn't shared the name we had chosen with anyone yet. My husband and I knew too well that people are kinder when you tell them the already-chosen name of your baby than when you tell them a name while pregnant. We had landed on the name for our son because my husband worked in Mexico City with someone with the same name. When he called me from the job months before I was pregnant and asked me if I liked the name, I told him I loved it. We put it in our back pockets in case we had a boy someday.

When we pulled out the name again for this pregnancy, we hadn't even looked up the meaning. Without asking anyone about it or telling my friend that we had picked a name, she had pulled and read me a card about the angel Rafael. She said that Rafael was the healing angel that came after Gabriel. Rafael was also the name that, months earlier, we had fallen in love with for our son. Rafael was born a few months after that and that is exactly what he was, our healing angel.

In between losing a baby and getting pregnant again, I cried a lot, I mourned a lot, and I talked to people about my pain a lot. I realized that most women that I spoke to could relate in some way: they had faced difficulties getting pregnant or staying pregnant, or they had lost a child. One of those conversations happened when I signed up for a private sewing class during my grieving period. My instructor, a woman in her sixties, asked me what made me want to start sewing. I explained that I had been gifted an old sewing machine by my mother-in-law and I just wanted to learn how to use it. After getting more comfortable with her, I confessed to her that I had just gone through a miscarriage and felt like I needed something to distract myself.

"I miscarried in the eighth month. I had gestational diabetes—and back then the testing for it wasn't great. My baby got too big and died before my due date," she shared.

"That is horrible, I am so sorry," I said. There were no words I could craft to respond, so this scarce offering was the best I could come up with—but it wasn't even close to the condolence she deserved for a loss so sizable.

"The best way to heal from pain like that is to go and have another baby. That was the only thing that made me smile again," she said.

Back then, I knew she was right—and I hoped that I could. There are so many women who lose baby after baby, never to conceive a lasting pregnancy. I began talking to more and more women and noticed a common theme. Like me, after their loss, they wanted to create something that they had some control over. One woman said she kept painting pots over and over. Another planted an herb garden. A friend said she started baking. I took a sewing lesson; eventually, I figured out how to sew, but I wasn't very good at it, and the skill wasn't enough to process my grief. What healed me the most—before I could even think about getting pregnant again—was talking with, connecting to, and hearing other people's stories.

I had felt so alone with my loss, but so many others had gone through it before me, and this cycle continues on and on. I wanted to create a project that, in some ways, shed light on how universal this loss is. My hope is that, if someone has suffered from a loss like the people's stories in this book, reading it would offer them some hope and healing.

Acknowledgements

When I miscarried days before my second trimester, Laura Dine Million was the first person I called. She had suffered multiple miscarriages specifically in her eleventh week of pregnancy. She never found out why but eventually when she made it past that eleventh week and through a healthy pregnancy, she didn't need to find out the answers anymore. She had a baby. I called her because she was the only person I knew who had experienced the same weight of having your hopes drop. I hoped she could lend me her voice, share her experience with me, and any advice she had for coping after such a loss. She did all that and more for me, and through talking to her I learned that the only way to feel less alone in my loss was to connect to others. It was from this place that Carry On was conceived.

To say none of this would be possible without David Andreone is a major understatement. He is the one who got me pregnant in the first place, so without *that*, this book would have never come to fruition. He is also my best friend and my love and has held my hand through so much. He was by my side for every bump in the road, and there were many on the way to us becoming parents. He has been up for reading, re-reading, proofreading, editing, uploading, and reviewing all along the way. He gets excited and enthusiastic with and for me, even when I am not. I am very grateful to him for all that and so much more.

I call my family every day. They live in New York and despite or because of the distance between us, I call them to feel a bit closer. That didn't change when I tried to have a baby. For every challenge, there was my check-in from Los Angeles. For every disappointment, there was a reminder not to get discouraged. My father

Lester Bart and sister Rachel Bart read anything and everything I sent them. They were honest and supportive, even when I sent messy first drafts. My brother, Aaron Bart couldn't wait to meet his new niece, and my mom, Amy Bart flew into the hospital room when I finally had a baby and has been celebrating every moment since. Although it would be nice to be able to hop in a car and see family, I'll settle for Facetime and a flight in between visits.

Although my in-laws are no longer alive, they were a big part of the reason my husband and I were able to get through trying to start a family of our own. My mother-in-law, Barbara Andreone, was so knowledgeable medically and was able to calmly and gently remind me that I was safe even when I was terrified. My father-in-law, Victor Andreone, waited patiently for an eighth grandchild from us and every hiccup along the way was met with his endless love.

My friends Andrea, Catherine, Lorin, and Orit were all there for me for the big stuff. Amiee and Adriana, no matter how long we are apart we always pick up where we left off. Thank you both for asking me when this book is coming out and that you can't wait to read it. Liz, unlucky for us but lucky us that we had Hyperemesis at the same time and had each other. I count my blessings in the friend department. Most of us were single when we met and we have seen each other through a lot of breakups, a lot of jobs, apartment moves, hardships, and heartaches. Your shoulders were quite wet from all the tears I have cried on them. We have come out the other side quite nicely, friends. I was there to watch two of you give birth, I took one of you to freeze your eggs, and one of you was there with me when I gave birth. It hasn't always been a walk in the park. Sometimes we have these crazy monumental hikes to climb, but thank goodness we have each other to help pull us up the mountain.

There was a certain way that I thought this process was going to go. I had an idea and an opinion with certain expectations of creating a published book. I knew so little and two people shed some light on what I didn't know I didn't know. Tara Jean O'Brien sat across from me at lunch and continued to support me even when I just had some barely formed beginnings of a book. She figured it out and was able to encourage me to do the same. Terence Michael opened my eyes to creating, polishing, and producing one's own work. He has done it three times over. and patiently shared with me all the details of what worked and what did not. He opened my eyes and changed my mind when I thought I couldn't do this. He answered question after question and helped me create a clear road map to follow.

This book would not have been possible without the people who shared their stories with me. The people who shared their struggles and devastation, the people who were vulnerable and felt hopeless, I thank you for talking about the hard stuff. This book is for you and for the many people like you who haven't spoken up yet and feel so alone. You are not alone.

Lastly, I am lucky enough to answer to "Mama" or "Mommy" from Annabelle and Rafael, my children. It is a privilege to have the honor of raising you. I couldn't be prouder of the people you are now and who I am witnessing you become. I do not for a second take for granted how hard it was to have you both. I am grateful to play my favorite and most important role as your mother.